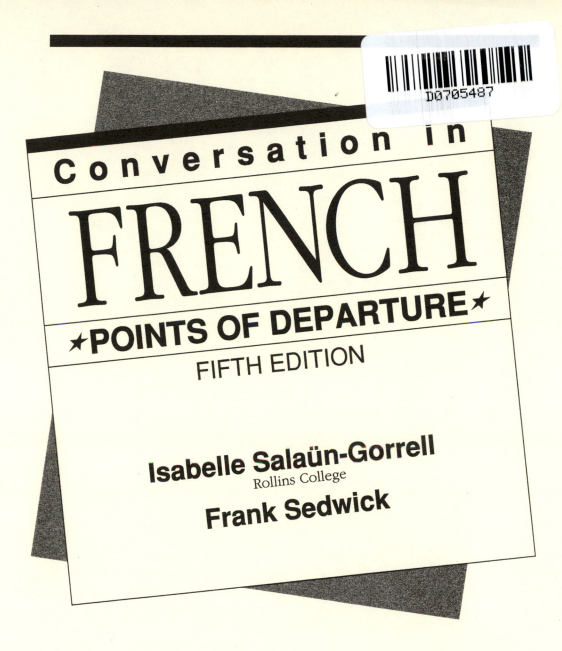

Conversation in
FRENCH
★POINTS OF DEPARTURE★
FIFTH EDITION

Isabelle Salaün-Gorrell
Rollins College

Frank Sedwick

HH⌐ Heinle & Heinle Publishers, Inc.
Boston, Massachusetts 02116, U.S.A.

Publisher: Stanley J. Galek
Editorial Director: Kristin Swanson
Assistant Editor: A. Marisa French
Production Manager: Erek Smith
Production Coordinator: Patricia Jalbert
Internal text design: Mia Saunders
Cover illustration and design: Jean Craig-Teerlink
Illustrations: Cary
Additional illustrations for this edition: Len Shalansky

Manufactured in the U.S.A.

ISBN: 0-8384-1716-7

10 9 8 7 6 5 4 3 2 1

Preface

CONVERSATION IN FRENCH: POINTS OF DEPARTURE, FIFTH EDITION, is designed for conversation and composition on nearly any level, even as early as the second semester of French. The difference among levels will lie in the degree of syntactic sophistication and richness of vocabulary in the student's response.

The Fifth Edition contains fifty-two scenes, grouped arbitrarily. The scenes represent everyday situations, experiences, and types of people to which the students can relate. Where differences of custom exist, many of these are either evident in the picture itself or are noted in the textual material; the instructor may want to supply others. We have eliminated two topics from the previous edition and added three new units from earlier editions (*"La vie en plein air", "Au port"* and *"Au zoo")* and their accompanying illustrations. Most units and their illustrations have been updated to reflect changes in custom, dress, and the cost of living. Most important, to every unit we have added a new and creative type of exercise called *"Imaginons et discutons!"*

CONVERSATION IN FRENCH is designed for flexibility and simplicity. Begin anywhere. Skip around among the units, backward or forward, as you wish. No progressive degree of difficulty is intended and no unit depends on any other. The specific vocabulary for each scene is self-sustaining for that lesson, so that there is no need for a vocabulary at the end of the book. Omit whatever units may not be pertinent to the condition or interests of the class. One scene and its apparatus, if pursued in their entirety, easily provide sufficient material for a one-hour class.

The title of the book with its reference to "points of departure" suggests the expansive way in which the various scenes should be used, with free and inventive response to pictorial suggestion. All of the situations are as modern, universal, and youth-oriented as possible and are cast into a series of questions and exercises whose aim is to expand conversations from, rather than limit them to, the picture at hand.

Each unit has a picture, a word list pertinent to that picture, a set of questions analyzing the picture, a set of "points of departure" questions utilizing the given vocabulary but not necessarily the picture, three suggested topics for discourse or composition, and a role-play situation designed to promote creative language practice. This last exercise, called *"Imaginons et discutons!"* is devised to enhance the flexible nature of the book and is new to the Fifth Edition. The materials assume that students have been exposed to basic French grammar and have at their command a fundamental vocabulary (although an appendix of numbers, verb tenses, and irregular verbs is useful at any level, and so is included here). The commonest words are taken for granted. Depending on the degree of intensity with which the book is used, it may be helpful for students to have a dictionary.

The word list in each lesson always includes three groupings: (1) verbs; (2) adjectives and expressions; (3) nouns. Every word in the list is used somewhere in the exercises or its use is occasioned somewhere in the most likely answers to the questions. A few users of past editions have suggested an alphabetization of this list. We have preferred not to do this for several reasons, mainly that all groupings in each list are logical and orderly as they stand, and not at all haphazard. Alphabetization would not facilitate reference in *"Le calendrier"* lesson, for example, where the days of the week are conveniently grouped, as are holidays. Another example is the grouping of eating utensils for easy recognition and association with one another in the unit on *"Le couvert."* Besides, alphabetization would create some awkward, even comical, sequences of words.

With the exception of common words, all questions use only the vocabulary of their own unit, as does the simplest form of their possible replies. The questions always total twenty, divided between the two types, *"Analyse de l'illustration"* and *"Points de départ."* No question is answerable only by "yes" or "no," though many of the first set of questions can be answered briefly. The *"Points de départ"* questions require more thoughtful replies, in many cases rather detailed ones. Preparation of the responses to the questions may be either written or oral but should be done outside the classroom. Additional questions will occur to the instructor as the class is in progress, for it is through spontaneous repartee that the aim of this book is accomplished.

The three topics for written or oral discourse in *"Sujets de discussion"* may be corrected either orally in class or handed to the instructor for individual annotation. Each student should choose one theme, because not all of the three topics in any given lesson will appeal to or be answerable by everybody. Of the three topics, there is always at least one that requires little imagination or linguistic accomplishment, and another one calculated to challenge the ingenuity of the best student. The list of words of any given unit is normally sufficient to meet the needs of at least one of these themes. Themes written in the first person do not necessarily have to be true, for at all times students are urged to combine imaginative inventiveness with linguistic skills and the vocabulary at their disposal.

The new and final exercise, *"Imaginons et discutons,"* presents a problem in English that students must act out and solve creatively in French. The situation is based on a language function and incorporates the theme and vocabulary of the lesson. This exercise is best done in pairs or small groups and should be prepared beforehand, so that students can think it through. Each pair or group should be encouraged to present the solution to the class. This sort of *commedia dell'arte* can be entertaining and convert a reticent class into a lively one.

We acknowledge with thanks the comments and suggestions of the many users of earlier editions who have taken the time to let us know about their classroom experiences with CONVERSATION IN FRENCH. This book was originally written in 1968 and published in 1969 with a print order of only two thousand copies—which sold out in a couple of weeks. The same book, updated through the years like this Fifth Edition, is now en route to a million copies in its five languages. Few foreign-language textbooks have proved so durable, so it is time to thank you for sharing our notion of how to approach a conversation-composition class.

Table des matières

Avis aux Étudiants

Voici une liste des mots qui seront utilisés fréquemment dans les leçons qui suivent, de façon à éviter trop de répétitions. Vous connaissez certainement plusieurs de ces mots. Sinon, nous vous conseillons de les apprendre maintenant. Nous recommandons également que vous fassiez une révision des conjugaisons, des verbes irréguliers les plus courants et des nombres; consultez l'appendice.

acheter to buy
s'acheter to be bought, buy for oneself
aimer bien to like
apercevoir to notice
appeler to name; to call
s'asseoir to sit down
attendre to wait
s'attendre à to expect
avoir l'air de to seem to (+ *inf.*), to look like (+ *noun*)
avoir lieu to happen, take place
boire to drink
choisir to choose, select
coûter to cost
décrire to describe
écrire to write
espérer to hope
être en train de (+ *inf.*) to be in the process of (+ *gerund*), to be (+ *gerund*)
expliquer to explain
garder to keep
lire to read
manger to eat
ouvrir to open
paraître to seem, appear
payer to pay
penser to think; to mean
plaire to please
porter to wear; to carry
préférer to prefer
savoir to know
sembler (+ *inf.*) to seem to (+ *inf.*)
se servir de to use, make use of
se trouver to be, be located
utiliser to use
vendre to sell
vouloir to want

l'arrière-plan *(m.)*, **le second plan** background
l'avantage *(m.)* advantage
le bras arm
le but purpose
la description description
le dessin picture
le devoir duty
la différence difference
l'enfant *(m.)* child
la façon way
le garçon boy
le genre kind, type
l'illustration *(f.)* illustration
l'image *(f.)* picture
l'inconvénient *(m.)* disadvantage
la jeune fille girl
le jour day
la main hand
le méthode way
la nuit night
l'objet *(m.)* object
la partie part
la personne person
la place place
la plupart de most, the majority of
le premier plan foreground
le problème problem
la ressemblance, la similarité similarity
la sorte kind, type

américain(e) American
aujourd'hui today
bas (basse) low
chaud(e) hot
court(e) small *(of things)*, short
derrière behind
au-dessus over
devant in front of
difficile hard, difficult
à droite (to the) right
européen (européenne) European
facile easy
froid(e) cold
à gauche (to the) left
en général, généralement in general
grand(e) tall *(of people)*, large
habituel (habituelle) usual
habituellement, en général usually
haut(e) tall *(of things)*
jamais never
jeune young
lent(e) slow
lentement slowly
nouveau (*before a vowel or mute* **h**, **nouvel**) (**nouvelle**) new
petit(e) small *(of people)*
près de at the side of, near
rapide fast
sous under
typique, classique typical
vieux (*before a vowel or mute* **h**, **vieil**) (**vieille**) old
vite, rapidement fast

to telephone **téléphoner**

to call, make a call **passer un coup de téléphone, passer un coup de fil**

to pick up a receiver **décrocher le récepteur**

to insert **introduire**

to dial a number **composer un numéro**

to wait **attendre**

to disturb **déranger**

to ask a question **poser une question**

to hear **entendre**

to hang up **raccrocher**

to cut off **interrompre**

to put through, connect **mettre en communication (avec)**

to make a long-distance call **passer un coup de téléphone, téléphoner à longue distance**

to dial "direct" **téléphoner directement**

to call information **demander les renseignements** (m.)

to accept the charges **accepter (de payer) la communication**

to look up **chercher**

certain **sûr(e)**

behind, after **derrière**

hello! **allô!**

the line is busy **la ligne est occupée**

expensive **cher (chère)**

convenient **pratique**

telephone **le téléphone**

receiver **le combiné**

telephone number **le numéro de téléphone**

coin **la pièce**

token **le jeton**

slot **la fente**

digit **le chiffre**

area code **l'indicatif téléphonique** (m.)

(telephone) call **le coup de téléphone, le coup de fil**

conversation **la conversation**

local call **la communication locale, la conversation locale**

station-to-station call **la communication téléphonique ordinaire**

person-to-person call **la communication téléphonique personnelle avec préavis**

long-distance call **la communication à longue distance**

dial tone **la tonalité**

party line **la ligne commune**

private line **la ligne privée**

phone card **la télécarte**

telephone booth **la cabine téléphonique**

switchboard **le standard**

operator **le (la) standardiste, l'opérateur (opératrice)**

telephone book **l'annuaire** (m.)

telephone bill **la note de téléphone**

minimum charge **le tarif minimum**

at less cost **à prix réduit**

minute **la minute**

lamp **la lampe**

wire **le fil**

father **le père**

Au téléphone

1

Analyse de l'illustration

1. Sur ce dessin, qui téléphone? À qui passe-t-il un coup de fil?
2. D'où le jeune homme téléphone-t-il?
3. Dans quelle main la jeune fille tient-elle le combiné? Et le jeune homme?
4. À votre avis, quel genre de conversation est en train d'avoir lieu?
5. Qu'y a-t-il derrière la jeune fille?

Points de départ

6. Quel est votre numéro de téléphone?
7. Combien de chiffres y a-t-il dans l'indicatif téléphonique de votre numéro?
8. Pourquoi une communication personnelle avec préavis coûte-t-elle plus cher qu'une communication téléphonique ordinaire?
9. À moins que vous ne puissiez téléphoner directement, à qui devez-vous parler pour passer un coup de téléphone à longue distance?
10. Combien coûte une communication locale dans votre région?
11. Quand vous avez composé le numéro et que la ligne est occupée, que faites-vous?
12. Que faites-vous quand un coup de téléphone est interrompu?
13. Décrivez un annuaire et dites ce qu'il contient.
14. Préférez-vous une ligne commune ou une ligne privée? Pourquoi?
15. Décrivez en détail ce que vous faites quand vous téléphonez d'une cabine téléphonique.
16. Vous voulez donner un coup de fil à quelqu'un, mais vous n'avez pas le numéro. Que faites-vous?
17. Pensez-vous qu'il soit intéressant d'avoir une télécarte? Quels en sont les avantages et les inconvénients?
18. À quel moment entendons-nous la tonalité?
19. Quand peut-on téléphoner à prix réduit?
20. Quand demande-t-on les renseignements?

Sujets de discussion

1. Mon père et la note de téléphone.
2. Avantages et inconvénients du téléphone.
3. Une conversation au téléphone.

★ ★
Imaginons et discutons!
★

From a telephone booth in Bordeaux, a person has placed a long-distance call to 78-31-54-60. When the number rings, someone in Lyon picks up the receiver and says, "Allô!" At this instant the call is cut off. The caller then dials the operator.

Enact the described situation in French.

to live **habiter**
to be sitting **être assis**
to study **étudier**
to listen (to) **écouter**
to play *(a musical instrument)* **jouer de**
to ski **faire du ski**
to smoke **fumer**
to wear **porter**
to annoy, bother **gêner**

(at the same) time **(en même) temps**
approximately **à peu près**
untidy, dirty **mal tenu(e), sale**
neat, clean **propre**
quiet **tranquille**
noisy **bruyant(e)**
besides **en plus**
disgusting **dégoûtant(e)**
unhealthy **malsain(e)**

room **la chambre**
dormitory **la résidence**
roommate **le (la) camarade de chambre**
student **l'étudiant(e)**
window **la fenêtre**
window sill **le rebord de la fenêtre**
can **la canette**
glasses **les lunettes** *(f. pl.)*
wall **le mur**
lamp **la lampe**
light **la lumière**
bed **le lit**
blanket **la couverture**
bookcase **l'étagère** *(f.)*
desk **le bureau**
book **le livre**
bunk bed **le lit gigogne**
notebook **le carnet**
pencil **le crayon**
wristwatch **le bracelet-montre**
watch **la montre**
pyjamas **le pyjama**

guitar **la guitare**
radio **la radio**
poster **l'affiche** *(f.)*
cigarette **la cigarette**
cigarette butt **le mégot**
pack of cigarettes **le paquet de cigarettes**
(cigarette) lighter **le briquet**
ash tray **le cendrier**
key **la clef**
key ring **le porte-clefs**
winter **l'hiver** *(m.)*
snow **la neige**
ski **le ski**
life **la vie**

Les camarades de chambre (hommes)

2

Analyse de l'illustration

1. Des deux compagnons de chambre, lequel est en train d'étudier?
2. Lequel des deux joue de la guitare?
3. Qu'y a-t-il sur le bureau?
4. Que voyez-vous sur le rebord de la fenêtre?
5. Que pensez-vous de cette chambre?
6. Qui a un crayon et où se trouve ce crayon?
7. Comment savez-vous que c'est la nuit et non pas le jour?
8. Où sont les affiches? Décrivez-les.
9. Que porte le jeune homme aux lunettes?
10. Qui a un bracelet-montre et où est-il?
11. Comment savez-vous que quelqu'un a fumé?
12. Il y a quelques livres sur le bureau. Y en a-t-il d'autres? Où sont-ils?

Points de départ

13. Pouvez-vous écouter la radio et étudier en même temps? Expliquez.
14. Fumez-vous? Justifiez votre réponse.
15. Qu'est-ce qu'il y a sur votre bureau dans votre chambre?
16. Préférez-vous étudier dans la journée ou le soir? Pourquoi?
17. Avez-vous des affiches sur les murs de votre chambre? Si oui, décrivez-les. Si non, pourquoi n'en avez-vous pas?
18. Peut-on faire du ski où vous habitez? Si oui, quand? Si non, pourquoi pas?
19. Pensez-vous que notre illustration d'une chambre d'étudiants soit typique? Pourquoi?
20. Aimeriez-vous que votre camarade de chambre joue d'un instrument de musique?

Sujets de discussion

1. La vie avec un(e) camarade de chambre.
2. Ma chambre à l'université.
3. La bonne ou la mauvaise façon d'étudier.

Imaginons et discutons!

Two friends who room together and usually get along well have started an argument about study-time and annoying personal habits. One objects to the other's guitar-playing during study-time and failure to keep the room clean. The other is annoyed by the noise of the radio and the cigarette smoke. At this point two of their friends appear in the open doorway.

Enact the described situation in French.

to wear **porter**
to fit the dress **épingler la robe**
to pin the hem **faire un ourlet**
to measure **prendre les mesures (de)**
to put, place **mettre**
to put up **coller**
to set one's hair **se faire une mise en plis**
to look (at) **regarder**
to remember **se souvenir (de)**
to need **avoir besoin (de)**
to notice **apercevoir**
to serve (as) **servir à**
to get along well (with) **s'entendre bien (avec)**
to go out **sortir**
to ask a question **poser une question**

useful **utile**
tall **grand(e)** *(people)*; **haut(e)** *(things)*
practical **pratique**

room *(habitation)* **la chambre, la pièce**	sandal **la sandale**	tape recorder **le magnétophone**
room *(space)* **la place, l'espace** *(m.)*	slacks **le pantalon**	photograph **la photo, la photographie**
roommate **le (la) camarade de chambre**	leg **la jambe**	(indoor) plant **la plante d'intérieur**
boyfriend **le petit ami**	stockings **les bas**	doll **la poupée**
girlfriend **la petite amie** *(for a boy)*; **l'amie** *(for a girl)*	panty hose **le collant**	life **la vie**
	door **la porte**	object **l'objet** *(m.)*
hair *(on the head)* **le cheveu** *(pl. les cheveux)*	mirror **le miroir**	mouth **la bouche**
	lamp **la lampe**	use **l'usage** *(m.)*, **l'emploi** *(m.)*
curler *(for the hair)* **le bigoudi, le rouleau**	window **la fenêtre**	yard *(measurement)* **le yard**
	curtain **le rideau**	yardstick, tape measure **le mètre**
pin **l'épingle** *(f.)*	rug **le tapis**	size, height **la taille**
pin box **la boîte d'épingles**	carpet **la maquette**	inch **le pouce**
dummy **le mannequin**	sofa **le canapé, le divan**	foot **le pied**
coat hanger **le cintre**	desk **le bureau**	meter **le mètre**
dress **la robe**	book **le livre**	centimeter **le centimètre**
skirt **la jupe**	letter **la lettre**	
zipper **la fermeture éclair**	stationery **le papier à lettres**	
hem **l'ourlet** *(m.)*	envelope **l'enveloppe** *(f.)*	
shoe **la chaussure**	bulletin board **le tableau d'affichage** *(m.)*	
	notice **la note**	
	record-player **le tourne-disque**	

Les camarades de chambre (femmes)

3

Analyse de l'illustration

1. Que fait la jeune fille qui a des épingles à la bouche?
2. Pourquoi la boîte d'épingles se trouve-t-elle sur le tapis?
3. À quoi sert le mètre?
4. Où se trouve le miroir et qui s'y regarde?
5. À votre avis, combien de jeunes filles habitent ensemble dans cette chambre?
6. Qui porte un pantalon? Qui porte des sandales? Et qui porte des chaussures?
7. Où y a-t-il quelques livres?
8. Que fait la jeune fille assise au bureau? A qui peut-elle bien écrire à votre avis?
9. Combien de photos voyez-vous et où sont-elles?
10. Quels objets peut-on apercevoir entre la porte et la lampe?
11. Où est le cintre et pourquoi est-il là?
12. Pensez-vous que cette illustration soit typique d'une chambre de jeune filles? Pourquoi?

Points de départ

13. Quand préférez-vous porter une robe plutôt qu'un pantalon?
14. Pensez-vous qu'il soit pratique d'avoir un tableau d'affichage dans sa chambre? Pourquoi?
15. Quand vous faites-vous une mise en plis? Expliquez.
16. Comment fait-on un ourlet?
17. Quand et à qui écrivez-vous des lettres?
18. Combien de pouces y a-t-il dans un pied et combien de pieds dans un yard?
19. Quelle est votre taille en pieds et en pouces?
20. Quelle est votre taille en mètres et en centimètres? (1 mètre = 3,3 pieds; 1 centimètre = 0,39 pouces)

Sujets de discussion

1. Ma chambre à l'université.
2. La vie avec mon (ma) camarade de chambre.
3. Sortir avec mon (ma) petit(e) ami(e).

★ ★

Imaginons et discutons!

★

Three roommates, who get along well but need more space, are discussing how to arrange their possessions and the objects in the room to make it more livable. Suddenly there is a knock at the door.

Enact the described situation in French.

to lecture **faire une conférence,
faire un cours magistral**
to attend lectures **suivre des cours**
to register (at the university)
s'inscrire (à l'université)
to major (in) **se spécialiser (en)**
to demonstrate **faire une
démonstration**
to take notes **prendre des notes**
to teach **enseigner**
to study **étudier**
to take an examination **passer un
examen**
to be successful, succeed **réussir**
to pass the examination **réussir à
l'examen** *(m.)*, **être reçu**
to fail *(intrans.)* **échouer**
to fail *(trans.)* **rater**
to name **nommer**
to interest **intéresser**
to take an interest in **s'intéresser à**
to distinguish **distinguer**

Spanish **espagnol(e)**
English **anglais(e)**
German **allemand(e)**
French **français(e)**
high **haut(e)**
low **bas, basse**
right-handed **droitier (droitière)**
left-handed **gaucher (gauchère)**
pleasant **agréable**
unpleasant **désagréable**
happy **content(e)**
on the subject of **au sujet de**

student **l'étudiant(e)**
professor **le professeur** (*no fem.:*
elle est professeur)
college, university **l'université** *(f.)*
high school **le lycée, le collège**
course, subject of instruction
le cours, la matière
major field **la matière principale**
class **le cours, la classe**
classroom **la classe**
explanation **l'explication** *(f.)*
lecture **la conférence**
lecture hall **la salle de conférences,
l'amphithéâtre, l'amphi** *(m.)*
skull **le crâne**
bench **le banc**
blackboard **le tableau noir**
building **le bâtiment, l'immeuble**
(m.)
model, mock-up **la maquette**
bridge **le pont**
chalk **la craie**
glasses **les lunettes** *(f. pl.)*

anatomy **l'anatomie** *(f.)*
architecture **l'architecture** *(f.)*
engineering **l'ingénierie** *(m.)*
literature **la littérature**
writer **l'écrivain** *(m.)* (*no fem.:* **elle
est écrivain**)
face **le visage**
number **le nombre**
enthusiasm **l'enthousiasme** *(m.)*
lot, heap **le tas (de)**

Les salles de conférences

4

Analyse de l'illustration

1. Qui porte des lunettes? Sur quels dessins?
2. Comment pouvez-vous distinguer le cours d'anatomie des autres cours?
3. Dans la salle où vous voyez sur une table la maquette d'un bâtiment, que fait le professeur?
4. Qui donne une explication au sujet d'un pont?
5. Qu'enseignent les professeurs?
6. Dans quels cours est-il impossible de voir le visage des étudiants?
7. Pourquoi est-il impossible de voir le visage du professeur d'architecture?
8. Quelle est la différence entre les bancs du cours d'anatomie et ceux du cours d'ingénierie?
9. Quel cours a le plus petit nombre d'étudiants?
10. Lequel des quatre cours vous intéresse le plus? Pourquoi?
11. Sur l'illustration, qui est gaucher? Comment le savez-vous?

Points de départ

12. Qui était Shakespeare?
13. Qu'est-ce qu'il y a d'agréable dans la vie d'un(e) étudiant(e)?
14. Quels sont les aspects désagréables de la vie d'un(e) étudiant(e)?
15. Avec quoi écrit-on sur le tableau?
16. Quand prend-on des notes?
17. En général, quelle est la différence entre une classe et un amphithéâtre?
18. Aimeriez-vous devenir professeur? Si oui, pourquoi? Si non, pourquoi pas?
19. Quelles différences y a-t-il entre le lycée et l'université?
20. Combien de matières étudiez-vous maintenant? Nommez-en deux.

Sujets de discussion

1. Pourquoi je ne veux pas échouer à mon examen.
2. Description de mon cours de …
3. Mon professeur préféré.

★ ★

Imaginons et discutons!

★

There are sixteen students in the class. Eight passed the exam, eight did not. Each had an explanation, all different, for having passed or failed. Start a group discussion in French that presents all sixteen explanations.

to read **lire**
to write **écrire**
to look (at) **regarder**
to browse, leaf through **feuilleter,**
  parcourir
to look up **chercher**
to lend **prêter**
to borrow **emprunter**
to find **trouver**
to stand (at) **se tenir (à, devant)**
to study **étudier**
to take notes **prendre des notes**
to go out **sortir**
to indicate **indiquer**
to thank **remercier**
to watch **observer**

fictional **fictif (fictive)**
nonfictional **documentaire, factuel**
  (factuelle)
imaginary **imaginaire**
true **vrai(e), véritable**
noisy **bruyant(e)**
quiet **silencieux (silencieuse)**
long **long (longue)**
short **court(e)**
bald **chauve**
lately **récemment, dernièrement**
briefly **brièvement**
yesterday **hier**
hardly any **presque pas, très peu**

library **la bibliothèque**
librarian **le (la) bibliothécaire**
professor **le professeur** (*no fem.:*
  elle est professeur)
teacher **le (la) maître (maîtresse)**
  (*kindergarten*) **l'instituteur**
  (**institutrice**) (*elem. school*)
magazine **le magazine**
dictionary **le dictionnaire**
word **le mot**
student **l'étudiant(e)**
pupil, student (*precollege*) **l'élève**
  (*m. and f.*)
book **le livre**
bookshelf, shelf **le rayon**
bookshelves **les étagères**
definition **la définition**
encyclopedia **l'encyclopédie** (*f.*)
information **l'information** (*f.*),
  le renseignement
atlas **l'atlas** (*m.*)
reference book **le livre de**
références

fiction **la fiction**
nonfiction **la littérature**
  documentaire, factuelle
artistic work **l'œuvre** (*f.*)
novel **le roman**
short story **la nouvelle**
poetry **la poésie**
plot **l'intrigue** (*f.*)
poem **le poème**
play **la pièce, la pièce de théâtre**
briefcase **la serviette,**
  le porte-documents
paper **le papier**
glasses **les lunettes** (*f. pl.*)
chair **la chaise**
skirt **la jupe**
slacks **le pantalon**
jeans **le jean**
sweater **le chandail, le sweater**
hand **la main**
foot **le pied**
shoe **la chaussure**

hair (*on the head*) **le cheveu** (*pl.* **les**
  cheveux)
boy, young fellow **le jeune homme**
little boy **le petit garçon**
girl, young unmarried woman
  la jeune fille
room **la chambre, la pièce**
little girl **la petite fille**
majority (of), most **la plupart (de)**

À la bibliothèque

5

Analyse de l'illustration

1. Combien de personnes sont visibles sur ce dessin?
2. Que font la plupart des étudiants et des étudiantes?
3. Qui est en train de sortir et que tient cette personne à la main?
4. Qui a les cheveux longs? Les cheveux courts? Qui est presque chauve?
5. Où sont la plupart des livres?
6. Comment savez-vous que c'est une bibliothèque?
7. Décrivez l'étudiante au premier plan.
8. Que fait la jeune fille devant les étagères?
9. Que fait l'étudiante aux cheveux longs?

Points de départ

10. Qu'est-ce qu'une bibliothèque?
11. Quelles sont les activités d'un(e) bibliothécaire?
12. En général, où préférez-vous étudier, à la bibliothèque ou dans votre chambre? Pourquoi?
13. Nommez quelques-unes des différences entre un livre et un magazine.
14. Expliquez la différence entre un dictionnaire et une encyclopédie.
15. Qu'est-ce qu'un livre de références? Nommez deux livres de références.
16. Expliquez la différence entre la fiction et la littérature documentaire.
17. Décrivez brièvement l'intrigue d'une nouvelle ou d'un roman que vous avez lu(e).
18. Que veut dire «feuilleter»?
19. Pourquoi ne doit-on pas écrire dans les livres de bibliothèque?
20. Décrivez la bibliothèque de votre école ou de votre université.

Sujets de discussion

1. Ce que l'on trouve dans une bibliothèque.
2. Étudier à la maison ou à la bibliothèque.
3. Un bon livre que j'ai lu récemment.

Imaginons et discutons!

A student cannot find a certain reference book on the shelf. Since the library does not lend reference books, it is probably in use. With the librarian's help the book is found on a table, where another student is leafing through the book and taking notes. When the two students agree to use the book together, the librarian leaves, but only briefly, as their conversation becomes too noisy.

Enact the described scene in French.

to dance **danser**
to sing **chanter**
to stay out late **rentrer tard**
to appear to (+ *inf.*) **avoir l'air
(*m.*) de (+ *inf.*)**
to have fun, enjoy oneself **bien
s'amuser**
to play a waltz **jouer une valse**
to play (*musical instrument*) **jouer
de**
to play a record **mettre un disque**
to play out of tune **jouer faux**
to smile **sourire**
to laugh **rire**
to hire **louer**
to take a break **faire une pause**
to check one's coat at the cloak room
**déposer son manteau au
vestiaire**
to return home **rentrer**

happy **heureux (heureuse)**
scratched **rayé(e)**
tardy, late **tardif (tardive)**
fast **rapide**
slow **lent(e)**

dance **le bal, la soirée dansante,
la boum**
discotheque **la discothèque**
nightclub **la boîte de nuit,
le night-club**
(individual) dance **la danse**
decorations **les décorations** (*f. pl.*)
band **l'orchestre** (*m.*)
bandstand **l'estrade** (*f.*)
cloak room **le vestiaire**
stereo **la stéréo**
record **le disque**
break, intermission **la pause**
pitcher **la cruche, le pot**
glass **le verre**
tray **le plateau**
sandwich **le sandwich**
beverage, drink **la boisson**
refreshments **les rafraîchissements**
(*m. pl.*)
musician **le (la) musicien
(musicienne)**

musical instrument **l'instrument
(*m.*) de musique**
guitar **la guitare**
drum **le tambour**
wind instrument **l'instrument** (*m.*) **à
vent**
trumpet **la trompette**
trombone **le trombone**
clarinet **la clarinette**
saxophone **le saxophone**
rhythm, tempo **le rythme**
waltz **la valse**
rock (and roll) **le rock (and roll)**
classical music **la musique classique**
semiclassical music **la musique
légère**
popular music **la musique populaire**
folk music **la musique folklorique**
teenager **l'adolescent(e),
le «teenager»**
background music **la musique
d'ambiance**

country music **la musique
folklorique**
partner (*at a dance*)
le (la) partenaire
wall **le mur**
mouth **la bouche**
bracelet **le bracelet**

La boum

6

1. Qu'y a-t-il comme rafraîchissements?
2. Quel genre de musique l'orchestre semble-t-il jouer? Qu'est-ce qui vous fait penser cela?
3. Décrivez les musiciens et ce qu'ils font.
4. D'après le dessin, les jeunes gens ont-ils l'air de bien s'amuser? Pourquoi?
5. Décrivez le couple au premier plan.
6. Voyez-vous des jeunes filles qui portent des bracelets? Lesquelles?
7. Sur le dessin, quels sont les jeunes gens qui ne dansent pas?
8. Qu'est-ce qu'un vestiaire et où est-il sur le dessin?
9. Où sont les décorations? et les musiciens?
10. Décrivez le dessin d'une façon générale.

Points de départ

11. Quand vous allez danser avec un garçon (ou une jeune fille) que vous ne connaissez pas bien, de quoi parlez-vous?
12. Quelle est la différence entre une valse et le rock?
13. Préféreriez-vous danser dans une boîte de nuit ou aller à une boum? Justifiez votre choix.
14. Quelle ressemblance existe-t-il entre une trompette, une clarinette, un saxophone et un trombone?
15. Quelle est l'heure la plus tardive à laquelle vous soyez rentré(e) chez vous? Quand était-ce et pourquoi?
16. Quel est l'instrument de musique le plus employé dans la musique folklorique?
17. De quel âge à quel âge est-on adolescent(e)?
18. Où peut-on laisser son manteau avant d'entrer dans la salle où l'on danse?
19. Comment est-il possible pour des jeunes gens de danser sans louer un orchestre?
20. Que peut-on faire quand l'orchestre fait une pause?

Sujets de discussion

1. Genres de musique.
2. Ce qui se passe quand je rentre trop tard.
3. Description d'une soirée dansante mal organisée.

Imaginons et discutons!

Your friends invite you to a party featuring your favorite local band. After dancing all night you and some others are invited to meet the musicians.

Enact the described scene in French.

to sit down **s'asseoir**
to be sitting **être assis**
to knit **tricoter**
to fall asleep **s'endormir**
to sleep **dormir**
to watch TV **regarder la télé**
to turn on (TV) **allumer**
to turn off (TV) **éteindre**
to advertise **faire de la publicité**
to have just (read) **venir de (lire)**
to hold **tenir**
to occur **se passer**
to exist **exister**
to listen **écouter**

while **tout en**
comfortably **confortablement**
favorite **préféré(e); favori (favorite)**
bad **mauvais(e)**
boring **ennuyeux (ennuyeuse)**
instructive **instructif (instructive)**

family **la famille**
father **le père**
mother **la mère**
son **le fils**
daughter **la fille**
husband **le mari, l'époux**
wife **la femme, l'épouse**
niece **la nièce**
nephew **le neveu**
grandfather **le grand-père**
grandmother **la grand-mère**
granddaughter **la petite-fille**
grandson **le petit-fils**
brother **le frère**
sister **la sœur**
aunt **la tante**
uncle **l'oncle**
cousin **le (la) cousin (cousine)**
relative *(family)* **le (la) parent(e)**
house, home **la maison**
home **le foyer, le chez soi**
window **la fenêtre**
table **la table**

sofa **le divan, le canapé**
lamp **la lampe**
armchair **le fauteuil**
furniture **les meubles** *(m. pl.)*
television set **le téléviseur**
television **la télévision, la télé**
color television **la télévision en couleur**
channel **la chaîne**
program **l'émission** *(f.)*
preference **la préférence**
film **le film**
TV news **le journal télévisé**
television "commercial" **la publicité, la «pub»**
station **la station**
radio **la radio**
radio (set) **le poste de radio**
transistor radio **le transistor**
daytime **la journée**
evening **la soirée**
scene **la scène**
portrait **le portrait**

size **la taille**
magazine **la revue, le magazine**
glasses **les lunettes** *(f. pl.)*
lap **les genoux** *(m. pl.)*
slipper **la pantoufle, le chausson**
pastime **le passe-temps**

La famille

7

Analyse de l'illustration

1. À votre avis, quel lien de parenté existe-t-il entre les quatre personnes?
2. À quelle heure de la journée ou de la soirée cette scène se passe-t-elle?
3. Que fait la mère en regardant la télé et où est-elle assise?
4. Décrivez les meubles du salon.
5. Est-ce que le père est assis confortablement? Comment le savez-vous?
6. Que fait le petit garçon et où est-il assis?
7. Où est le téléviseur?
8. Comment savez-vous que le père vient de lire?
9. Pourquoi le père s'est-il endormi à votre avis?

Points de départ

10. Quel est votre passe-temps préféré quand vous êtes chez vous le soir?
11. En parlant de radio ou de télévision, quelle est la différence entre une chaîne et un poste?
12. Quelle est votre émission de télévision préférée? Si vous n'avez pas de préférence, expliquez pourquoi.
13. Qu'est-ce qu'une publicité?
14. Où et quand aimez-vous écouter la radio?
15. Décrivez votre famille.
16. Faites en quelques mots le portrait de votre parent(e) favori (favorite).
17. Qui êtes-vous pour la soeur de votre père? pour la fille de votre grand-père? pour la fille du frère de votre mère? pour votre oncle?
18. Regardez-vous souvent le journal télévisé? Pourquoi?
19. Quand écoutez-vous la radio? Quelle station préférez-vous?
20. Expliquez la différence entre une «maison» et un «chez soi».

Sujets de discussion

1. Pourquoi, en général, j'aime (je n'aime pas) la télévision.
2. Soirée en famille à la maison.
3. Mon foyer et ma famille.

Imaginons et discutons!

A family is seated in the living room after dinner. Suddenly their attention is captured by a television commercial that starts a discussion among all members of the family.

Enact this discussion in French.

to make the bed **faire le lit**
to clean the house **faire le ménage**
to dust **essuyer, épousseter**
to sweep **balayer**
to vacuum **passer l'aspirateur**
to scrub **frotter fort**
to rent, hire **louer**
to buy **acheter**
to own **posséder**
to keep *(preserve)* **garder**
to live **habiter**
to play *(musical instr.)* **jouer de**
to notice **apercevoir**
to perform *(work)* **effectuer**

roomy **spacieux (spacieuse)**
loose, pell-mell **en vrac**

house **la maison**
home **le foyer, l'intérieur**
"dream home" **la maison de mes rêves**
two-story house **la maison à deux étages**
housewife **la ménagère**
household chores **les travaux ménagers**
upper floor **l'étage** *(m.)* **supérieur**
groundfloor **le rez-de-chaussée**
basement **le sous-sol**
cellar **la cave**
floor plan **le plan de la maison**
stairway **l'escalier** *(m.)*
attic **le grenier**
roof **le toit**
apartment **l'appartement** *(m.)*
chimney **la cheminée**
lightening rod **le paratonnerre**
window **la fenêtre**
doorway **la porte**
ceiling **le plafond**

wall *(interior)* **le mur**
room **la pièce**
living room **le salon**
dining room **la salle à manger**
bedroom **la chambre à coucher**
bathroom **la salle de bains**
kitchen **la cuisine**
floor *(to walk on)* **le plancher**
floor *(unit of counting)* **l'étage** *(m.)*
corridor **le couloir, le corridor**
piano **le piano**
buffet, sideboard **le buffet**
rug **le tapis**
lamp **la lampe**
fireplace **la cheminée**
furniture **les meubles, le mobilier**
knick-knack **le bibelot**
portrait **le portrait**
piece of furniture **le meuble**
chest of drawers **la commode**
desk **le bureau**
chair **la chaise**
armchair **le fauteuil**

footstool, hassock **le repose-pieds, le pouf**
cushion **le coussin**
planter **la jardinière**
trunk **la malle**
curtain **le rideau**
drape **le double rideau**
furnace **la chaudière**
garbage can **la poubelle, la boîte à ordures**
down payment **les arrhes** *(f. pl.)*
maid **la femme de ménage**

La maison

8

1. Combien d'étages cette maison a-t-elle?
2. Quelles pièces voyez-vous?
3. Que voyez-vous dans le grenier?
4. Où se trouvent les poubelles?
5. Où apercevez-vous un tapis?
6. Qu'y a-t-il sur le toit?
7. Décrivez ce que vous voyez dans la salle à manger.
8. Où est la cuisine?
9. Aimeriez-vous habiter dans cette maison? Pourquoi? Pourquoi pas?
10. Où sont les fauteuils devant lesquels il y a des poufs?
11. Où est la salle de bains que l'on aperçoit?
12. Où se trouve l'escalier?
13. Que fait le petit garçon?
14. Quels meubles apercevez-vous dans la pièce où il y a un bureau?

Points de départ

15. Nommez quelques travaux que la ménagère doit effectuer chaque jour.
16. Qu'y a-t-il dans une cave en général?
17. Pourquoi beaucoup de gens louent-ils un appartement au lieu d'acheter une maison?
18. Pourquoi beaucoup de gens aiment-ils mieux acheter une maison que louer un appartement?
19. Qu'est-ce que les gens gardent généralement dans leurs malles et en vrac au grenier?
20. Expliquez ce que sont les arrhes.

Sujets de discussion

1. La maison de mes rêves.
2. Ce que j'ai trouvé dans un vieux grenier.
3. Comment je fais le ménage chez moi.

Imaginons et discutons!

A group of tourists is visiting a famous home. As the visitors enter each room, they express their opinions and compare thoughts on their own dream houses.

Enact this discussion in French.

to cook *(tr.)* **préparer, faire cuire**
to cook *(intr.)* **faire la cuisine,**
    cuisiner
to cook *(of food)* **cuire**
to uncork **déboucher**
to pour **verser**
to serve **servir**
to be hungry **avoir faim**
to be very hungry **avoir très faim**
to reach **atteindre**
to scold **gronder**
to prevent (from) **empêcher (de)**
to wash dishes **faire la vaisselle**
to place **placer**
to sit down **s'asseoir**
to pass **passer**
to get cold **refroidir**

good *(for s.o.)* **bon** *(pour + acc.)*
delicious **délicieux (délicieuse)**
tasteless **insipide**
above **au-dessus**

mother **la mère**
father **le père**
son **le fils**
daughter **la fille**
housewife **la maîtresse de maison**
kitchen **la cuisine**
meal **le repas**
garbage disposal **le broyeur à**
    ordures
kitchen appliance **l'appareil** *(m.)*
    ménager
food processor **le robot-ménager**
stove **la cuisinière**
electric stove **la cuisinière**
    électrique
hood **la hotte**
burner **la plaque chauffante,**
    le brûleur
back burner **la plaque arrière**
front burner **la plaque de devant**
oven **le four**
microwave oven **le four à**
    micro-ondes

sink **l'évier** *(m.)*
refrigerator **le réfrigérateur**
dishwasher **le lave-vaisselle**
cupboard **le placard**
window sill **le rebord de la fenêtre**
basket **le panier**
bread **le pain**
toaster **le grille-pain**
roll **le petit pain**
coffee **le café**
coffee pot **la cafetière**
(coffee) cup **la tasse**
salad **la salade**
salad bowl **le saladier**
fruit stand **la coupe de fruits**
apple **la pomme**
salt **le sel**
pepper **le poivre**
vinegar **le vinaigre**
oil **l'huile** *(f.)*
bottle **la bouteille**
pan **la casserole**
ladle **la louche**

pot **la marmite, la casserole**
frying pan **la poêle**
dish **le plat**
glass **le verre**
wine **le vin**
cork **le bouchon**
fruit **le fruit**
plate **l'assiette** *(f.)*
napkin **la serviette**
meal **le repas**
food **la nourriture**
flower pot **le pot à fleurs, le pot de**
    fleurs
dishwashing soap **le liquide**
    vaisselle

18

Dans la cuisine

9

Analyse de l'illustration

1. Qui a l'air d'avoir très faim? Comment le savez-vous?
2. Qu'est-ce que le père a à la main et que fait-il?
3. Quels appareils ménagers ne sont pas visibles sur ce dessin?
4. Sur quelle plaque de la cuisinière la cafetière se trouve-t-elle?
5. Quand servira-t-on le café? Comment le savez-vous?
6. Que voyez-vous sur le rebord de la fenêtre?
7. Quel genre de fruits y a-t-il sur la table?
8. Dans quoi les a-t-on placés?
9. Que fait la jeune fille? Pourquoi?
10. Comment savez-vous que le vin a été débouché, mais pas encore servi?
11. Qui va boire du vin et qui ne va pas en boire?   Comment le savez-vous?
12. Qu'est-ce qu'il y a dans les petites bouteilles à gauche du saladier?
13. S'il s'agit d'une scène européenne, quand mangera-t-on les fruits?
14. Où est le saladier? Où sont le poivre et le sel?
15. Qu'y a-t-il au-dessus du réfrigérateur?

Points de départ

16. Décrivez votre cuisine.
17. À quoi sert un panier à pain?
18. Quand mange-t-on la salade en Amérique? et en Europe? Quand préférez vous la manger?
19. Pourquoi aimez-vous (ou n'aimez-vous pas) manger dans la cuisine?
20. Que préférez-vous faire: préparer le repas ou faire la vaisselle? Expliquez pourquoi.

Sujets de discussion

1. Dialogue entre une cuisinière électrique et un four à micro-ondes.
2. Avantages et inconvénients du lave-vaisselle.
3. Cuisines d'hier et d'aujourd'hui.

Imaginons et discutons!

At dinnertime in a typical home we might expect the mother to prepare the meal, the father to serve it, and the children to fight at the table. But imagine all members of the family in the illustration on the previous page to have reversed the stereotype.

Enact the dialog at the table in French.

to shave (oneself) **(se) raser**
to throw away **jeter**
to clean (brush) one's teeth **se laver (brosser) les dents**
to turn on the water **ouvrir le robinet**
to turn off the water **fermer le robinet**
to take a bath **prendre un bain**
to take a shower **prendre une douche**
to pull **tirer**
to dry (oneself) **(se) sécher**
to run (*of water*) **couler**
to run water **faire couler de l'eau** (*f.*)
to splash **éclabousser**
to wash (oneself) **(se) laver, faire sa toilette**
to wear **porter**
to live **vivre, habiter**
to get electrocuted **se faire électrocuter**

alone **seul(e)**
close (to) **près (de)**
everywhere **partout**
dangerous **dangereux (dangereuse)**
convenient **pratique**

bathroom **la salle de bains**
wife **l'épouse**
husband **le mari**
bottle **le flacon** (*perfume, etc.*)
garment **le vêtement**
bathrobe **le peignoir**
pajamas **le pyjama**
towel **la serviette**
towel rack **le porte-serviette**
washbowl **le lavabo**
counter (*bathroom*) **le comptoir**
faucet **le robinet**
soap **le savon**
toothbrush **la brosse à dents**
toothpaste **le dentifrice**
disposable razor **le rasoir jetable**
electric razor **le rasoir électrique**
plug **la prise**
cord **le fil électrique, le cordon**
end **le bout**
shaving cream **la crème à raser**
mirror **le miroir**
glass (*container*) **le verre**

ceiling **le plafond**
(tile) floor **le carrelage**
(on the) floor **(par) terre** (*f.*)
toilet **les toilettes, les W.C.**
bidet **le bidet**
bathtub **la baignoire**
shower **la douche**
shelf **l'étagère** (*f.*)
(shower) curtain **le rideau (de douche)**
(electrical) outlet **la prise (de courant)**
rug **le tapis**
air vent **la bouche d'aération**

Dans la salle de bains

Analyse de l'illustration

1. Comment savez-vous que l'homme se prépare à prendre un bain et non pas une douche?
2. Cette salle de bains, est-elle américaine ou européenne? Comment le savez-vous?
3. Qu'y a-t-il par terre?
4. Où se trouvent les serviettes?
5. Où est la prise de courant?
6. Où se trouve la bouche d'aération?
7. Quels objets y a-t-il à la droite de l'homme qui se rase? Qu'y a-t-il devant lui?
8. Où sont les toilettes?
9. Quelle sorte de vêtement l'homme porte-t-il?
10. Que voyez-vous au premier plan?
11. Sur cette illustration, quels sont les objets qui vous font penser que cet homme ne vit probablement pas seul?
12. Pourquoi ne voyez-vous pas de crème à raser?
13. Pourquoi est-il dangereux de se raser avec un rasoir électrique près d'un lavabo?

Points de départ

14. À quoi servent les serviettes?
15. Expliquez la fonction d'un rideau de douche.
16. Comment se lave-t-on les mains? Expliquez en détail.
17. Deux hommes veulent prendre une douche et se raser. Quelle est la première chose que chacun fera, si l'un a un rasoir électrique et l'autre un rasoir jetable?
18. Combien de fois par jour vous lavez-vous les dents?
19. Quelle est la différence entre une baignoire et un lavabo?
20. En général, préférez-vous prendre un bain ou une douche? Pourquoi?

Sujets de discussion

1. Salles de bains anciennes et modernes.
2. Rasoirs jetables et rasoirs électriques.
3. Faire sa toilette.

★ ★
Imaginons et discutons!

★

Four students who share two dormitory rooms and one bathroom are discussing ways to improve their general living conditions. Central to their discussion is the use of and responsibility for the bathroom.

By enacting their discussion in French, help them come up with a schedule for use and maintenance of the bathroom.

to set the table **mettre la table, mettre le couvert**
to clear the table **débarrasser la table, desservir**
to serve **servir**
to pour **verser**
to make toast **faire du pain grillé, faire des toasts**
to make a toast *(to someone or something)* **porter un toast (à quelqu'un ou à quelque chose)**
to have just (done it) **venir de (le faire)**
to celebrate **célébrer**
to make a blunder **faire un faux-pas**

formal **cérémonieux (cérémonieuse)**
informal **sans cérémonie**
everybody **tout le monde**
on the subject of **au sujet de, à propos de**
on the left side **à gauche**
during **pendant, lors de**
in the French way **à la française**

table **la table**
etiquette **le savoir-vivre, les règles *(f. pl.)* de bienséance *(f.)*, l'étiquette *(f.)***
meal **le repas**
dinner *(supper)* **le dîner**
gala dinner **le dîner de gala**
tablecloth **la nappe**
napkin **la serviette**
center piece **la corbeille de fleurs**
anniversary **l'anniversaire *(m.)***
head of the table **la tête de la table**
place setting **le couvert**
cutlery, silverware **l'argenterie *(f.)***
plate **l'assiette *(f.)***
saucer **la soucoupe**
dinner knife **le couteau (de table)**
butter knife **le couteau à beurre**
dinner fork **la grande fourchette**
salad fork **la fourchette à salade**
dessert fork **la fourchette à dessert**
teaspoon **la petite cuillère**

soup spoon, tablespoon **la cuillère à soupe, la grande cuillère**
saltshaker **la salière**
peppershaker **le poivrier**
soup bowl **la soupière**
decanter **la carafe**
water **l'eau *(f.)***
wine **le vin**
wine basket **la corbeille à vin**
water glass **le verre à eau**
wine glass **le verre à vin**
ash tray **le cendrier**
cigarette **la cigarette**
(cigarette) lighter **le briquet**
flower **la fleur**
host **l'hôte**
hostess **l'hôtesse**
guest **l'invité(e)**
waiter **le garçon**
waitress **la serveuse**
duties **les fonctions *(f. pl.)***
tray **le plateau**

chair **la chaise**
maid **la bonne**

Le couvert

11

Analyse de l'illustration

1. Comment savez-vous que le repas n'a pas encore été servi?
2. Qu'est-ce qui vous indique qu'il s'agit d'un grand dîner?
3. Que versera-t-on dans chacun des deux verres?
4. Quelle est la différence entre la grande fourchette et la petite fourchette?
5. Cette table a-t-elle été mise à la française ou à l'américaine?
6. Pourquoi chaque couvert a-t-il une petite cuillère et une cuillère à soupe?
7. Où sont placées les serviettes?
8. Qu'est-ce qu'il y a au milieu de la table?
9. Qui va s'asseoir en tête de table?
10. S'il y a deux hôtes, combien d'invités vont venir pour dîner?
11. Quels couverts voyez-vous à droite de chaque assiette?
12. Où sont la salière et le poivrier?
13. À quoi sert la petite assiette à gauche de chaque couvert?
14. Pourquoi les corbeilles à vin sont-elles dans cette position?
15. Qu'y a-t-il devant les couverts des deux hôtes?
16. Quand tout le monde sera assis, qui aura la carafe à sa gauche?

Points de départ

17. Comment porte-t-on un toast à quelqu'un?
18. Quelles sont les fonctions d'un garçon ou d'une serveuse?
19. Quelle est la différence entre une assiette et une soucoupe? entre une grande cuillère et une petite cuillère?
20. Que préférez-vous: un grand dîner ou un dîner sans cérémonie? Pourquoi?

Sujets de discussion

1. La façon de mettre le couvert à l'américaine.
2. Conversation entendue lors d'un grand dîner.
3. Faire un faux-pas lors d'un dîner de gala.

Imaginons et discutons!

After enjoying a formal meal served on an elegantly-set table in a French home, it is now time for the guests to relish in some after-dinner conversation along with one more glass of a special French wine. With compliments to the host and hostess, and several toasts, much of the attention centers on the guest of honor.

Enact the described scene in French and include as many guests as you like.

to breathe **respirer**
to bend *(intr.)* **se plier, se baisser**
to run **courir**
to close **fermer**
to link **joindre**
to enumerate **énumérer**
to call **appeler**
to function **fonctionner**
to find **trouver**
to consist of **se composer de**
to see **voir**
to circulate **circuler**
to be called **s'appeler, se nommer**

human **humain(e)**
healthy *(good for you)* **sain(e)**
healthy *(in good health)* **en bonne santé**
unhealthy *(bad for you)* **malsain(e)**
in bad health **en mauvaise santé**
tall **grand(e)** *(people)*; **haut(e)** *(things)*
short **petit(e)** *(people)*; **court(e)** *(things)*
physical **physique**
visible **visible**
below **en dessous, au-dessous**
above **en dessus, au-dessus**
thin, slender **mince**
skinny **maigre**
heavy **lourd(e)**
fat **gros (grosse)**
young **jeune**
old **vieux (vieil) (vieille)**
married **marié(e)**
single **célibataire**
right **droit(e)**
left **gauche**
similar **semblable**
from the front **de face**
from the back **de dos**
sideways **de côté**

body **le corps**
attitude **l'attitude** *(f.)*
face **le visage**
head **la tête**
forehead, brow **le front**
skull **le crâne**
brain **le cerveau**
hair **le cheveu** *(pl.* **cheveux**)
hair *(other than head)* **le poil**
eye **l'œil** (*m. pl.* **les yeux**)
eyelid **la paupière**
eyelash **le cil**
eyebrow **le sourcil**
ear **l'oreille** *(f.)*
hearing **l'ouie** *(f.)*
nose **le nez** *(pl. unchanged)*
cheek **la joue**
jaw **la mâchoire**
mouth **la bouche**
lip **la lèvre**
tongue **la langue**
tooth **la dent**
chin **le menton**

beard **la barbe**
neck **le cou**
trunk *(of the body)* **le torse**
shoulder **l'épaule** *(f.)*
back **le dos**
chest *(men or women)* **la poitrine**
breast *(women)* **la poitrine, le sein**
arm **le bras**
elbow **le coude**
wrist **le poignet**
hand **la main**
palm **la paume**
finger **le doigt**
thumb **le pouce**
index finger **l'index** *(m.)*
middle finger **le majeur**
ring finger **l'annulaire** *(m.)*
little finger **l'auriculaire** *(m.)*
ring **la bague; l'anneau** *(m.)*
mustache **la moustache**
fingernail **l'ongle** *(m.)*
fist **le poing**
waist **la taille**

hip **la hanche**
buttock **la fesse**
thigh **la cuisse**
leg **la jambe**
knee **le genou**
calf **le mollet**
ankle **la cheville**
foot **le pied**
toe **l'orteil** *(m.)*, **le doigt de pied**
toenail **l'ongle** *(m.)* **de l'orteil, du doigt de pied**
heel **le talon**
bone **l'os** *(m., pl. unchanged)*
joint **la jointure, l'articulation** *(f.)*
skin **la peau**
blood **le sang**
artery **l'artère** *(f.)*
vein **la veine**
heart **le cœur**
stomach **l'estomac** *(m.)*
lung **le poumon**
muscle **le muscle**

Le corps humain

Analyse de l'illustration

1. Décrivez l'homme.
2. Décrivez la femme.
3. Comparez leur attitude.

Points de départ

4. Par quoi la tête est-elle jointe au torse?
5. Enumérez les différentes parties du visage.
6. Expliquez la différence entre un cil et un sourcil.
7. Que trouve-t-on dans le crâne?
8. Combien de dents un(e) adulte normal(e) a-t-il (a-t-elle)?
9. Chez une personne grosse, quelles sont les parties du corps les plus visibles?
10. Comment circule le sang?
11. Combien de doigts avons-nous?
12. Comment se nomment les cinq doigts en français?
13. Si vous portez une bague, au doigt de quelle main la portez-vous? Sinon, pourquoi n'en portez-vous pas?
14. Nommez une partie extérieure du corps sur laquelle il n'y a pas de peau.
15. Quelle est la fonction des poumons?
16. Quand nous courons, quelles parties du corps utilisons-nous?
17. De quoi se compose une main?
18. Quelles sont les parties du corps qui peuvent se plier?
19. Comment appelle-t-on une main fermée?
20. Nommez deux parties du corps qui sont seulement visibles de dos et deux qui ne sont visibles que de face.

Sujets de discussion

1. Comment fonctionne le corps humain.
2. Comment rester sain.
3. Hommes et femmes sur la planète Mars.

Imaginons et discutons!

Imagine that you have just witnessed a crime. In order to help the police find the suspect(s), you are asked to give complete physical description(s) to the composite artist, played by another student.

Enact the discussion in French between you and the artist.

to grow *(hair)* **pousser**
to cut hair **couper les cheveux**
to get a haircut **se faire couper les cheveux**
to wash **laver**
to rinse **rincer**
to have one's hair permed **se faire faire une permanente**
to dry **sécher**
to comb **peigner**
to comb (out) **démêler**
to roll *(hair)* on curlers **se mettre des rouleaux**
to dye **teindre**
to bleach **décolorer**
to tease hair **(se) crêper les cheveux**
to blow-dry one's hair **se faire un brushing**
to manicure **faire une manucure**
to contain **contenir**
to shave (oneself) **se raser**
to get a shave **se faire raser**

blond **blond (blonde)**
brunette **brune**
light brown **châtain**
red haired **roux (rousse)**
bald **chauve**
bearded **barbu**
moustached **moustachu**
short **court (courte)**
long **long (longue)**
tangled **emmêlé(e)**

beauty care **les soins de beauté**
barber **le coiffeur** *(pour hommes)*
customer **le (la) client(e)**
hair *(on the head)* **les cheveux** *(m., pl.)*
haircut **la coupe de cheveux**
hair dresser **le (la) coiffeur (coiffeuse)** *(pour dames)*
beauty parlor **le salon de beauté**
beautician **l'esthéticien (esthéticienne)**
comb **le peigne**
scissors **les ciseaux** *(m. pl.)*
soap **le savon**
razor blade **la lame de rasoir**
electric razor **le rasoir électrique**
after-shave lotion **la lotion après-rasage**
moustache **la moustache**
beard **la barbe**
sideburns **les pattes**
hair style **la coiffure**
shampoo **le shampooing**

dryer **le sèche-cheveux**
curler **le bigoudi**
roller **le rouleau**
hair pin **l'épingle** *(f.)* **à cheveux**
bobby pin **la pince à cheveux**
"set" **la mise en pli**
eyelash **le cil**
face **le visage**
eyeshadow **le fard à paupières**
mascara **le mascara**
bottle **le flacon** *(perfume, etc.)*
powder **la poudre**
lipstick **le rouge à lèvres**
hand cream **la crème pour les mains**
manicure **la manucure**
manicurist **le (la) manucure**
fingernail **l'ongle** *(m.)* **de la main**
nail file **la lime à ongles**
nail polish **le vernis à ongles**
nail polish remover **le dissolvant**
wig **la perruque**

Les soins de beauté

13

Analyse de l'illustration

1. Que fait le coiffeur dans l'illustration à gauche?
2. Que fait celui du salon de coiffure pour dames?
3. Que font les deux coiffeuses à l'arrière-plan du magasin?
4. Que contiennent les différents flacons que nous voyons sur trois des images?
5. Que fait la jeune femme devant le miroir?
6. Qu'admire le monsieur devant le miroir?

Points de départ

7. Qu'est-ce qu'un(e) coiffeur (coiffeuse) unisexe?
8. Dans un salon de coiffure, que fait le (la) coiffeur (coiffeuse) avant de vous peigner?
9. Que fait-on quand on a les cheveux emmêlés?
10. Expliquez ce que fait une manucure.
11. Que peut faire une brune qui désire être blonde ou rousse?
12. Comment vous maquillez-vous?
13. Sur quelle partie du visage met-on le fard à paupières? et le mascara?
14. Qu'est-ce qu'un shampooing?
15. Vous faites-vous souvent couper les cheveux? Expliquez pourquoi.
16. Décrivez vos cheveux.
17. Quelle différence y a-t-il entre la moustache, la barbe et les pattes?
18. Que peut acheter un homme qui est chauve?
19. Avec quoi préférez-vous raser? avec un rasoir de sûreté ou un rasoir électrique? Pourquoi?
20. Que peut faire une femme qui veut changer de style de coiffure?

Sujets de discussion

1. Discussion entre deux clientes dans un salon de beauté.
2. Changer de style de coiffure.
3. Les soins de beauté.

Imaginons et discutons!

After work, two hairdressers are discussing the day's events at the shop, including anecdotes about the clients and their requests.

Enact this discussion in French.

to play sports **faire du sport,**
    pratiquer un sport
to play (tennis, football, *etc.*) **jouer à**
    (au tennis, au football, *etc.*)
to attend **assister (à)**
to win **gagner**
to lose **perdre**
to throw **lancer**
to hit *(a ball)* **frapper**
to serve *(a ball)* **servir**
to score a point **marquer un point**
to run **courir**
to swim **nager**
to ski **faire du ski**
to take part in **participer à**
to be healthy **être en bonne santé**

inside, indoors **à l'intérieur**
violent **violent(e)**
in good shape **en bonne forme**

sport **le sport**
sports fan **le (la) passionné(e) de sport**
sports enthusiast **le (la) fanatique de sport**
athlete **l'athlète** *(m. and f.)*
amateur **l'amateur** *(m.)*
spectator **le (la) spectateur (spectatrice)**
professional **le (la) professionnel (professionnelle)**
game, match **la partie, le match, les matches**
player **le (la) joueur (joueuse)**
runner **le (la) coureur (coureuse)**
team **l'équipe** *(f.)*
referee, umpire **l'arbitre** *(m.)*
bad loser **le (la) mauvais(e) perdant(e)**
point **le point**
tie, draw **le match nul**
stadium **le stade**
court **le court**

field **le terrain**
line **la ligne**
ball **la balle**
singles **le simple**
doubles **le double**
tennis **le tennis**
racket **la raquette**
net **le filet**
soccer **le football**
goalkeeper **le (la) gardien (gardienne) de but**
goal **le but**
goal post **le poteau de but**
goal line **la ligne de but**
basketball **le basket-ball, le basket**
track and field **l'athlétisme**
track *(on which one runs)* **la piste**
race **la course**
finish *(of a race)* **l'arrivée** *(f.)*
football **le football américain**
baseball **le base-ball**
boxing **la boxe**
boxer **le boxeur**

heavyweight **le poids lourd**
ring **le ring**
golf **le golf**
golf club **le club de golf**
racketball **le racket-ball**
volleyball **le volley-ball**
swimming **la natation**
horseback riding **l'équitation** *(f.)*
wrestling **le catch**
fencing **l'escrime** *(f.)*
skating **le patinage**
skiing **le ski**
hockey **le hockey**
champion **le (la) champion (championne)**

Les sports

14

Analyse de l'illustration

1. Quels sont les quatre sports représentés sur le dessin?
2. Identifiez les balles et les filets qui sont visibles.
3. Le tennis: Pensez-vous que ceci soit une partie de simple ou de double? Pourquoi?
4. Le football: Quel joueur est le gardien de but?
5. Le courses: Qui va gagner (ou qui a déjà gagné)?

Points de départ

6. Qu'est-ce qu'un athlète?
7. Combien de joueurs faut-il avoir pour faire une partie de basket-ball?
8. De combien de joueurs se compose une équipe de football?
9. Pour quel sport doit-on se servir d'un animal?
10. Quels sports se jouent sur un court?
11. Expliquez ce qu'est un stade.
12. À votre avis, combien coûte une bonne raquette de tennis (ou un bon club de golf)?
13. Qu'est-ce qu'un(e) fanatique de football? Expliquez.
14. Nommez le champion de boxe poids lourd. Si vous ne pouvez pas le nommer, expliquez pourquoi.
15. Qu'est-ce qu'un match nul?
16. Quels sont les sports toujours pratiqués sur un ring?
17. Quels sports pratiquez-vous?
18. Quels sports aimez-vous regarder?
19. Que préférez-vous: les sports d'équipe ou les sports individuels? Pourquoi?
20. «L'important n'est pas de gagner ou de perdre, mais la façon de jouer.» Expliquez.

Sujets de discussion

1. Un mauvais(e) joueur (joueuse).
2. Les sports à mon école ou à mon université.
3. L'importance du sport dans la vie.

Imaginons et discutons!

The team has lost another game. At a meeting after the game, the players are discussing what went wrong. Each player has a different opinion.

Enact this discussion in French.

to have a picnic **faire un pique-nique, pique-niquer**
to park **garer**
to make a sandwich **faire un sandwich**
to spread (butter on bread) **tartiner**
to cut, slice **couper en tranches**
to uncork **déboucher**
to kneel **être à genoux**
to appear to (+ *inf.*) **avoir l'air de (+ *inf.*)**
to discard **jeter, mettre à la poubelle**
to forget **oublier**
to go back home **rentrer à la maison**
to find **trouver**
to take part **participer**
to contain **contenir**
to concern, be about **s'agir de**

pleasant **agréable**
unpleasant **désagréable**
shady **à l'ombre** (*f.*) , **ombragé(e)**
sunny **ensoleillé(e), au soleil**
great! **fantastique; chouette! super!**

picnic **le pique-nique**
picnicker **le (la) pique-niqueur (pique-niqueusse)**
car **la voiture**
grass **l'herbe** (*f.*)
tree **l'arbre** (*m.*)
ant **la fourmi**
fly **la mouche**
mosquito **le moustique**
picnic basket **le panier à pique-nique**
food supplies **les provisions**
loaf of bread **le pain**
piece (*slice*) of bread **la tranche de pain**
knife **le couteau**
sausage **la saucisse** (*to be cooked*) ; **le saucisson** (*salami*)
cheese **le fromage**
cheese sandwich **le sandwich au fromage**
wine **le vin**
bottle **la bouteille**

cork **le bouchon**
corkscrew **le tire-bouchon**
thermos jug **la bouteille thermos, le thermos**
beverage **la boisson**
soft drink **le soda, la boisson gazeuse**
paper cup **le gobelet en papier**
paper plate **l'assiette** (*f.*) **en papier**
aspect **l'aspect** (*m.*)
place, spot **l'endroit** (*m.*) , **le coin**
blanket **la couverture**

Le pique-nique

Analyse de l'illustration

1. Quels aspects du dessin vous font penser qu'il s'agit d'une scène européenne?
2. Où les pique-niqueurs ont-ils garé leur voiture?
3. Que fait le jeune homme qui est à genoux?
4. Que fait la jeune fille?
5. Que fait le jeune homme avec le couteau?
6. Qu'y a-t-il dans le panier à votre avis?
7. Décrivez l'endroit où les gens sont en train de pique-niquer.
8. De quoi semblent-ils parler?
9. Que tient chaque personne à la main gauche?
10. Qu'est-ce que chaque personne tient à la main droite?
11. Aimeriez-vous participer au pique-nique que vous voyez sur l'illustration? Pour quelles raisons?

Points de départ

12. Quels sont les aspects agréables d'un pique-nique?
13. Quels en sonts les aspects désagréables?
14. Préférez-vous un endroit au soleil ou à l'ombre pour faire un pique-nique? Pourquoi?
15. Comment faites-vous un sandwich au fromage?
16. Quel est l'avantage d'une bouteille thermos?
17. Quel est l'avantage des gobelets et des assiettes en papier?
18. Que feriez-vous à un pique-nique si vous aviez oublié le panier contenant les provisions et la boisson?
19. Que feriez-vous si vous trouviez des fourmis dans votre sandwich?
20. Quelles provisions prendrait-on pour un pique-nique américain?

Sujets de discussion

1. Pourquoi j'aime (je n'aime pas) pique-niquer.
2. Comment préparer un panier pour un pique-nique.
3. Un pique-nique que je n'oublierai jamais.

Imaginons et discutons!

A group of friends has arrived at the countryside for a day of picnicking. Their basket is full of food and drink, and their spirits are high. As the blankets are spread on the grass, something happens.

Enact the situation in French.

to swim **nager**
to float **flotter**
to sail **faire de la voile**
to surf, go surfing **faire du surf**
to water ski **faire du ski nautique**
to sunbathe **prendre un bain de**
   soleil, se faire bronzer
to put on suntan lotion **se mettre de**
   la lotion solaire
to get a tan **bronzer**
to dig **creuser**
to look at **regarder**
to play **jouer**
to warn **avertir**
to avoid **éviter**
to hand **passer, donner**
to hold **tenir**
to try **essayer**
to carry away **emporter**
to die **mourir**
to seem **avoir l'air** *(m.)*
to count **compter**

tanned **bronzé(e), hâlé(e)**
sometimes **parfois**
useful **utile**
amusing **amusant(e)**

beach **la plage**
ocean **l'océan** *(m.)*
sand **le sable**
shell **le coquillage**
lighthouse **le phare**
land **la terre**
wave **la vague**
surf **le ressac**
surfboard **la planche (de surf)**
rubber raft **le matelas pneumatique**
ship **le bateau**
sailboat **le voilier**
(beach) umbrella **le parasol**
towel **la serviette**
bath towel **la serviette de bain**
bath robe **le peignoir**
blanket **la couverture**
bathing suit **le maillot de bain**
bikini **le deux-pièces**
cap **la casquette**
hat **le chapeau**
bonnet **le bonnet**
pail **le seau**

shovel **la pelle**
thermos bottle **la bouteille thermos,**
   le thermos
carry-all, tote bag **le fourre-tout**
suntan lotion **la lotion solaire**
suntan creme **la crème solaire**
sunburn **le coup de soleil**
sunstroke **le coup de chaleur,**
   l'insolation *(f.)*
sunglasses **les lunettes** *(f. pl.)* **de**
   soleil
scarf **le foulard**
cup **le gobelet**
ball **la balle**
binoculars **les jumelles** *(f. pl.)*
radio **le poste de radio**
deck chair **la chaise longue**
usefulness, use **l'utilité** *(f.)*
life-guard **le maître-nageur** *(no*
   fem.: **elle est maître-nageur***)*

À la plage

Analyse de l'illustration

1. Il y a deux postes de radio sur l'illustration. Qui s'en sert, et où sont-ils?
2. Que semble vouloir faire la petite fille qui porte un bonnet?
3. Qui est en deux-pièces?
4. Que fait la dame assise sur la couverture?
5. Qu'est-ce que le monsieur avec les jumelles a l'air de regarder?
6. Que se disent le monsieur avec la casquette et la dame avec le foulard?
7. Qui a un matelas pneumatique et où a-t-il l'air de l'emporter?
8. Que font les jeunes gens qui sont à l'arrière plan à gauche?
9. Où voyez-vous un petit voilier?
10. Qui porte des lunettes de soleil?
11. Que peut-il y avoir dans le fourre-tout de la dame?
12. Où sont les coquillages?
13. Où sont les thermos?
14. Que semble dire le jeune homme à la jeune fille en deux-pièces?

Points de départ

15. Quelle est l'utilité d'un phare?
16. Pourquoi est-il utile d'emporter des jumelles à la plage?
17. Quelle est la différence entre un chapeau et une casquette?
18. Quelles sont les différentes façons d'éviter un coup de soleil quand on prend un bain de soleil?
19. Pourquoi est-il en général difficile de nager dans l'océan?
20. Allez-vous parfois à la plage? Sinon, pourquoi pas?

Sujets de discussion

1. Avantages et inconvénients d'être maître-nageur.
2. La plage n'est pas pour moi.
3. Les choses que l'on peut faire à la plage.

Imaginons et discutons!

While enjoying a sunny day on the beach, you and your friends see an empty raft floating to shore. You decide to tell the lifeguard on duty.

Enact the situation in French.

to cast *(a fishing line)* **lancer**
to fish with rod and line **pêcher à la ligne**
to shoot **tirer, tuer**
to shoot (at) **tirer (sur)**
to aim *(a gun)* **viser**
to hunt **chasser**
to climb **escalader**
to paddle **pagayer**
to fish (for) **pêcher**
to catch *(a fish)* **attraper**
to go camping **faire du camping**
to suspect **soupçonner**
to sing **chanter**
to take along **emporter**

red **rouge**
useful **utile**
along **le long de**

outdoor life **la vie en plein air**
fisher **le (la) pêcheur (pêcheuse)**
hunter **le chasseur**
camper **le campeur**
hiker **le (la) randonneur (randonneuse)**
canoe **le canoë**
fishing rod **la canne à pêche**
(fishing) line **la ligne**
reel **le moulinet**
fly casting **la pêche à la mouche**
fish **le poisson**
trout **la truite**
gun **le fusil**
deer **le cerf**
game bag **la carnassière, la gibecière**
canoe paddle **la pagaie**
stream **le ruisseau**
river **la rivière**
bow *(of a boat)* **la proue, l'avant**
stern *(of a boat)* **la poupe, l'arrière**
tent **la tente**

camp **le camp**
campfire **le feu de camp**
bonfire **le feu de joie**
fire **le feu**
sleeping bag **le sac de couchage**
campsite **le terrain de camping**
mountain **la montagne**
top **le haut, le sommet**
knapsack **le sac à dos**
hike **la randonnée**
garment **le vêtement**
hat **le chapeau**
skillet **la poêle**
season **la saison**
winter **l'hiver** *(m.)*
summer **l'été** *(m.)*
spring **le printemps**
fall **l'automne** *(m.)*

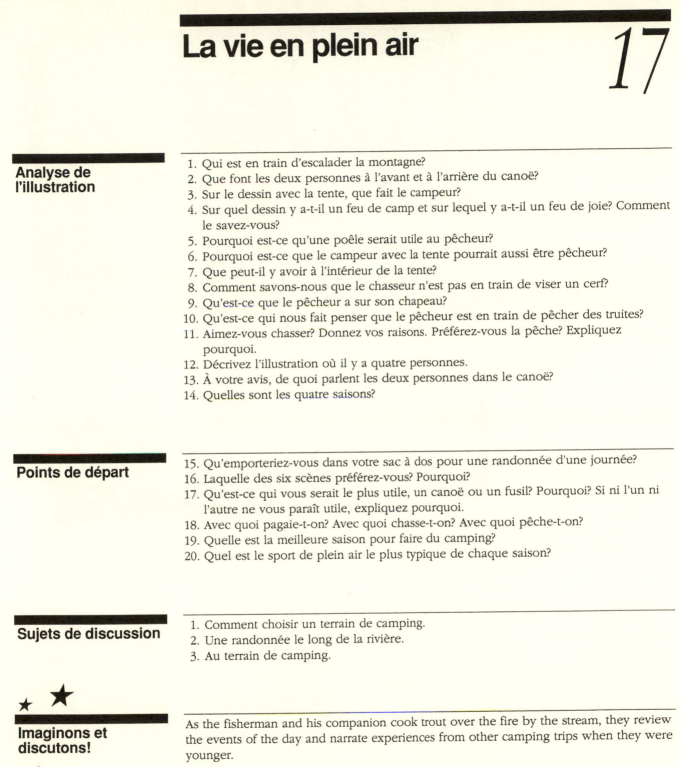

Analyse de l'illustration

1. Qui est en train d'escalader la montagne?
2. Que font les deux personnes à l'avant et à l'arrière du canoë?
3. Sur le dessin avec la tente, que fait le campeur?
4. Sur quel dessin y a-t-il un feu de camp et sur lequel y a-t-il un feu de joie? Comment le savez-vous?
5. Pourquoi est-ce qu'une poêle serait utile au pêcheur?
6. Pourquoi est-ce que le campeur avec la tente pourrait aussi être pêcheur?
7. Que peut-il y avoir à l'intérieur de la tente?
8. Comment savons-nous que le chasseur n'est pas en train de viser un cerf?
9. Qu'est-ce que le pêcheur a sur son chapeau?
10. Qu'est-ce qui nous fait penser que le pêcheur est en train de pêcher des truites?
11. Aimez-vous chasser? Donnez vos raisons. Préférez-vous la pêche? Expliquez pourquoi.
12. Décrivez l'illustration où il y a quatre personnes.
13. À votre avis, de quoi parlent les deux personnes dans le canoë?
14. Quelles sont les quatre saisons?

Points de départ

15. Qu'emporteriez-vous dans votre sac à dos pour une randonnée d'une journée?
16. Laquelle des six scènes préférez-vous? Pourquoi?
17. Qu'est-ce qui vous serait le plus utile, un canoë ou un fusil? Pourquoi? Si ni l'un ni l'autre ne vous paraît utile, expliquez pourquoi.
18. Avec quoi pagaie-t-on? Avec quoi chasse-t-on? Avec quoi pêche-t-on?
19. Quelle est la meilleure saison pour faire du camping?
20. Quel est le sport de plein air le plus typique de chaque saison?

Sujets de discussion

1. Comment choisir un terrain de camping.
2. Une randonnée le long de la rivière.
3. Au terrain de camping.

Imaginons et discutons!

As the fisherman and his companion cook trout over the fire by the stream, they review the events of the day and narrate experiences from other camping trips when they were younger.

Enact this dialog in French.

to wear **porter**
to display **exposer**
to consist of **consister de**
to have in common **avoir en commun**
to mark, state *(price)* **marquer**

single-breasted **droit(e)**
double-breasted **croisé(e)**
for sale **en vente, à vendre**
on sale *(special)* **en solde**
elegant **élégant(e)**
dressy **habillé(e)**
old-fashioned **démodé(e)**
fashionable **à la mode**
on display *(in the window)* **à l'étalage, en vitrine, à la devanture**

men's shop **le magasin pour hommes**
display window **l'étalage** *(m.)*, **la devanture, la vitrine**
clothing *(in general)*, apparel **les vêtements, l'habillement** *(m.)*
article of clothing **le vêtement**
attire, garb **les vêtements**
suit *(man's)* **le costume**
pants *(trousers)* **le pantalon**
suit jacket **le veston, la veste**
tie **la cravate**
bow tie **le nœud papillon**
shirt **la chemise**
sport shirt **la chemise sport**
long sleeves **les manches longues**
short sleeves **les manches courtes**
pocket **la poche**
hip pocket **la poche-revolver**
side pocket **la poche de côté**
inside pocket *(jacket)* **la poche intérieure**

breast pocket *(jacket)* **la poche de poitrine**
handkerchief **le mouchoir**
underwear **les sous-vêtements**
undershorts **le slip**
undershirt **le maillot de corps**
sock **la chaussette**
pair **la paire**
belt **la ceinture**
buckle **la boucle**
shoe **la chaussure**
wallet **le portefeuille**
cuff **la manchette**
cuff link **le bouton de manchette**
tie pin **l'épingle** *(f.)* **de cravate**
pullover *(sweater)* **le pull-over, le chandail**
jeans **le jean**
shoelace **le lacet**
collar **le col**
size **la taille, la pointure** *(for shoes, gloves, hats)*
button **le bouton**

monogram **le monogramme**
leather **le cuir**
dummy **le mannequin, la forme**
coat of arms **le blason**
price tag, label **l'étiquette** *(f.)*
birthday present **le cadeau d'anniversaire**

Le magasin pour hommes

Analyse de l'illustration

1. Décrivez les vêtements du mannequin.
2. Décrivez les vêtements des trois autres formes.
3. Décrivez les articles qui ne sont ni sur le mannequin ni sur les formes.
4. De tous les articles exposés, quel est probablement le moins cher?
5. Où est le monogramme sur la chemise sport?
6. Qu'est-ce qui n'est pas en vitrine, mais est porté tous les jours par la plupart des hommes?
7. Que porte le jeune homme devant la vitrine?
8. Pensez-vous que le blason soit à vendre?
9. De tous les vêtements que vous voyez dans la vitrine, quels sont ceux que la plupart des hommes ne portent pas tous les jours?
10. Quelle est la différence entre les chaussures du mannequin et les autres chaussures en vitrine?

Points de départ

11. Quelle est la différence entre les deux vestons que vous apercevez?
12. Qu'est-ce qu'une étiquette?
13. En quoi un costume consiste-t-il?
14. Quels sous-vêtements un homme porte-t-il?
15. Qu'est-ce qu'ont en commun une ceinture, un portefeuille et une paire de chaussures?
16. Quels vêtements d'homme peuvent avoir des boutons?
17. En général, combien de poches un pantalon a-t-il?
18. Si un américain porte un costume, où met-il son portefeuille, en général? Où le met un européen?
19. Pour pouvoir porter des boutons de manchettes et une épingle de cravate, quel genre de vêtements un homme doit-il porter?
20. En général, quelles sont les deux dimensions qu'un homme doit connaître pour s'acheter des chemises?

Sujets de discussion

1. Les vêtements que j'aime (que je n'aime pas) porter.
2. Comment arranger un étalage dans un magasin pour hommes.
3. Choisir un cadeau d'anniversaire pour un(e) ami(e).

★ ★

Imaginons et discutons!

★

Last night you dreamed you visited a men's shop to get some new clothes during a sale. Suddenly the mannequins came to life and started asking you questions and telling you what to wear!

Enact the dialog in French.

to shop **faire des achats, faire des courses**
to sell **vendre**
to spend *(money)* **dépenser**
to pay cash **payer comptant, payer en liquide**
to charge **mettre sur un compte**
to ring up a sale *(on the cash register)* **enregistrer une vente**
to look for **chercher**
to try on **essayer**
to fit, suit *(someone)* **aller (à quelqu'un)**
to open a charge account **ouvrir un compte**
to hold *(grasp)* **tenir**
to care about **tenir à**
to be right **avoir raison**
to happen, take place **se passer, arriver**
to argue **discuter**

authentic **authentique**
artificial **artificiel (artificielle)**
on display **à l'étalage, exposé(e)**
open **ouvert(e)**
expensive **cher (chère)**
fragile **fragile**
inexpensive **bon marché**
special (on sale) **en solde**
pretty **joli(e)**

department store **le grand magasin**
counter **le comptoir**
drawer **le tiroir**
cash register **la caisse**
mirror **le miroir**
showcase **la vitrine**
aisle **l'allée** *(f.)*
department **le rayon**
salesman **le vendeur**
saleswoman **la vendeuse**
customer, shopper **le (la) client(e)**
sale *(transaction)* **la vente**
clearance sale **les soldes**
article of clothing, garment **le vêtement**
size **la grandeur, la dimension, la taille, la pointure**
glove **le gant**
sweater **le pull-over, le sweater**
blouse **le chemisier**
skirt **la jupe**
fur coat **le manteau de fourrure**
stockings **les bas**

panty hose **le collant**
scarf **l'écharpe** *(f.)*
jewelry **la bijouterie**
costume jewelry **les bijoux fantaisie** *(m. pl.)*
necklace **le collier**
earring **la boucle d'oreille** *(f.)*
bracelet **le bracelet**
brooch **la broche**
leather goods **la maroquinerie**
purse **le sac à main**
flower **la fleur**

Dans le grand magasin

1. Que fait la cliente devant le rayon des fleurs artificielles?
2. Que cherche la vendeuse dans le tiroir ouvert?
3. Que fait la dame devant le miroir?
4. Quels articles sont exposés sur le comptoir au rayon bijouterie?
5. Pourquoi n'y a-t-il que des vendeuses et pas de vendeurs?
6. Que se passe-t-il au rayon des gants?
7. Est-ce un pullover ou un chemisier que la cliente tient devant elle? Pourquoi le tient-elle de cette façon?
8. Qu'ont l'air de se dire le client et la vendeuse au rayon maroquinerie?
9. Comment savez-vous que le sac à main près du miroir n'est pas à vendre?
10. Où est la caisse et que s'y passe-t-il?
11. Quel article sur ce dessin serait le plus difficile à acheter si la cliente ne connaissait pas sa taille? Pourquoi?
12. Enumérez tous les articles que vous voyez dans les vitrines.

Points de départ

13. Quel est l'avantage de mettre ce que l'on achète sur son compte?
14. Quel est l'avantage de payer comptant?
15. Qu'est-ce qu'un article en solde?
16. Qu'est-ce qu'un grand magasin?
17. «Le client a toujours raison.» Expliquez.
18. Pourquoi est-ce que les grands magasins demandent à leurs clients d'ouvrir des comptes?
19. Aimeriez-vous être vendeur (vendeuse) dans un grand magasin? Pourquoi (pas)?
20. La plupart des femmes aiment faire leurs achats dans un grand magasin: la plupart des hommes n'y tiennent pas. Croyez-vous que cela soit vrai? Pourquoi (pas)?

Sujets de discussion

1. Avantages et inconvénients des bijoux fantaisie.
2. Les grands magasins et les petites boutiques.
3. Comment je dépenserais $5000 dans un grand magasin.

★ ★

**Imaginons et
discutons!**

★

Bring to life the illustration on the preceding page. Enact in French any of the dialogs you imagine are taking place. Involve as many customers and/or sales personnel as you like.

to go grocery shopping **faire les courses, faire les commissions**

to shop *(in general)* **faire des courses, faire des achats**

to wait in line **faire la queue**

to contain **contenir**

to weigh **peser**

to pick up *(from floor)* **ramasser**

to add (up) the bill **faire le compte**

to slice **couper en tranches**

to peel **éplucher**

to suggest **suggérer**

to drop **laisser tomber**

to pack, put in a bag **mettre dans un sac**

to indicate, state *(price)* **marquer**

to fill **remplir**

to indicate **indiquer**

to be on sale **être en réclame, en promotion**

raw **cru(e)**

fresh **frais (fraîche)**

frozen **surgelé(e)** *(of foods)*

dear, expensive **cher (chère)**

per pound **la livre**

especially **surtout**

canned **en boîte**

supermarket **le supermarché**
shopper **le (la) client(e)**
shopping cart **le caddy**
checker **le (la) caissier (caissière)**
clerk *(store)* **l'employé(e)**
purse **le porte-monnaie**
counter **le comptoir**
purchase **l'achat** *(m.)*
cash register **la caisse**
paper bag **le sac en papier**
scale **la balance**
groceries **les produits d'alimentation, les aliments** *(m. pl.)*
check **le chèque**
food **la nourriture**
shopping *(grocery)* list **la liste d'achats**
bottle **la bouteille**
fruit **le fruit**
vegetable **le légume**
apple **la pomme**
banana **la banane**
peach **la pêche**
pear **la poire**

orange **l'orange** *(f.)*
grapefruit **le pamplemousse**
tomato **la tomate**
potato **la pomme de terre**
product **le produit**
carrot **la carotte**
celery **le céleri**
salad **la salade**
lettuce **la laitue**
spinach **les épinards** *(m. pl.)*
cabbage **le chou**
cauliflower **le chou-fleur**
zucchini **la courgette**
green beans **les haricots verts**
green peas **les petits pois** *(m. pl.)*
meat **la viande**
package **le paquet**
cheese **le fromage**
egg **l'œuf** *(m.)*
fish **le poisson**
beef **le bœuf**
veal **le veau**
lamb **l'agneau** *(m.)*
pork **le porc**

chop **la côtelette**
chicken **le poulet**
rice **le riz**
flour **la farine**
cookies **les petits gâteaux**
piece **le morceau**
butchery **la boucherie**
milk **le lait**
kilo *(2.2 lb.)* **le kilo**
pound *(.45 kilo)* **la livre**
liter *(1.06 quarts)* **le litre**
gram *(0.035 ounce)* **le gramme**
carton **le carton**
can **la boîte de conserve**
bag, sack **le sac**
apron **le tablier**
pencil **le crayon**
ear **l'oreille** *(f.)*
weight **le poids**
price **le prix**
week **la semaine**
vegetarian **le (la) végétarien (végétarienne)**

Au supermarché

Analyse de l'illustration

1. Qu'est-ce que l'enfant a l'air d'avoir fait?
2. Quels achats la cliente a-t-elle déjà faits? Comment le savez-vous?
3. Qui est l'homme avec le tablier et que fait-il?
4. Pourquoi le vendeur a-t-il un crayon derrière l'oreille? Que va-t-il faire avec ce crayon?
5. Que voyez-vous à l'arrière-plan à droite?

Points de départ

6. Aimez-vous faire vos courses au supermarché? Expliquez.
7. Qui fait les courses dans votre famille? Pourquoi?
8. Quels sont les produits les plus chers et les moins chers au supermarché?
9. Quels aliments peut-on acheter avec $20?
10. Quels fruits contiennent beaucoup de vitamine C?
11. Quel légume ne se mange jamais cru?
12. Qu'est-ce qui contient plus de lait: un gallon ou quatre litres? Expliquez votre réponse.
13. Combien de livres y a-t-il dans cinq kilos?
14. Quels fruits coupons-nous en tranches, en général? Quels légumes épluchons-nous?
15. Quels légumes peuvent se manger en salade?
16. Si vous achetez un morceau de bœuf, un poisson ou un poulet, lequel sera le moins cher à la livre et lequel sera le plus cher?
17. Nommez quelques aliments qui se vendent en boîtes.
18. Quand met-on tous ses achats dans un sac au supermarché?
19. Où, quand et pourquoi doit-on faire la queue au supermarché?
20. Expliquez le terme «végétarien».

Sujets de discussion

1. Ce que je vais manger aujourd'hui.
2. Quand je fais les courses au supermarché.
3. Avantages et inconvénients des produits surgelés.

Imaginons et discutons!

You and a friend are at the supermarket. As you two roam the aisles to choose your groceries, it becomes apparent that your eating habits are quite different.

Enact this situation in French.

to fill *(an order)* **exécuter**
to write a prescription **rédiger une ordonnance**
to make up, prepare **préparer**
to wait on (a customer) **s'occuper d'(un(e) client (cliente), servir**
to display **montrer, exposer, étaler**
to hand in **remettre**
to smell good **sentir bon**
to be visible **être en vue**
to stay open **rester ouvert(e)**
to find out **apprendre**
to contain **contenir**
to enumerate **énumérer**

behind **derrière**
for sale **en vente**
alternately, by turns **à tour de rôle, par roulement**
numerous **nombreux (nombreuse)**

drugstore **la pharmacie**
drugstore "on duty" **la pharmacie de service**
license **la license, le permis**
druggist, pharmacist **le (la) pharmacien (pharmacienne)**
prescription **l'ordonnance** *(f.)*
drug **la drogue**
medicine **le médicament**
(to have a) headache **(avoir) mal à la tête**
tablet **le cachet, le comprimé**
aspirin **l'aspirine** *(f.)*
doctor, physician **le docteur, le médecin** *(no f.:* **elle est docteur)**
contents **le contenu**
dose, dosage **la dose**
bottle **la bouteille, le flacon**
jar **le bocal, le pot**
box **la boîte**
soap **le savon**

bar of soap **la savonnette**

tube of toothpaste **un tube de dentifrice** *(m.)*
cosmetics **les produits** *(m.)* **de beauté** *(f.)*
perfume **le parfum**
cologne **l'eau de Cologne** *(f.)*
baby powder **le talc**
baby bottle **le biberon**
diaper **la couche culotte**
nail polish **le vernis à ongles**
nail-polish remover **le dissolvant à ongles**
shampoo **le shampooing**
sunglasses **les lunettes de soleil**
stick of chewing gum **le paquet de «chewing gum»**
pack (package) **le paquet**
cream **la crème**
suntan lotion **la lotion solaire**
vacation **les vacances** *(pl.)*
sea **la mer**

mountain **la montagne**
place **l'endroit** *(m.)*
wall **le mur**
year **l'année** *(f.)* **, l'an** *(m.)*
shelf **l'étagère** *(f.)*
price tag, label **l'étiquette** *(f.)*

À la pharmacie

Analyse de l'illustration

1. Enumérez quelques-uns des objets que vous voyez exposés.
2. Que peut contenir le flacon que la dame a dans la main?
3. Pourquoi la dame lit-elle l'étiquette?
4. Qu'est-ce que le pharmacien a l'air de faire?
5. Qu'apercevez-vous au premier plan, derrière la dame?
6. Pourquoi les médicaments à l'arrière plan ne sont-ils pas sur les étagères avec les produits de beauté?
7. Quels autres articles généralement en vente dans une pharmacie américaine typique ne voyez-vous pas sur cette illustration?
8. Qu'est-ce qui est bien en vue sur le mur derrière le pharmacien?
9. Pour qui le pharmacien prépare-t-il l'ordonnance à votre avis?
10. À votre avis que contiennent les flacons à gauche de l'illustration?

Points de départ

11. Quand un docteur rédige une ordonnance, à qui la remet-on pour la faire exécuter?
12. Qu'est-ce qu'une mère peut acheter pour son bébé dans une pharmacie?
13. Préférez-vous acheter vos produits de beauté en pharmacie ou dans un grand magasin? Pourquoi?
14. Qu'est-ce qu'une pharmacie de garde?
15. Les cachets sont mis dans des boîtes ou dans des flacons. Dans quoi met-on le dentifrice?
16. Que peut-on faire quand on a mal à la tête?
17. Quelle est la différence entre le savon et le shampooing?
18. Achetez-vous souvent du parfum? Pourquoi?
19. Avant de partir en vacances à la montagne ou à la mer, qu'achetez-vous en pharmacie?
20. Que faites-vous après que le médecin vous ait rédigé une ordonnance?

Sujets de discussion

1. Les différences entre une pharmacie américaine et une pharmacie européenne.
2. Les produits de beauté féminins.
3. Préféreriez-vous être docteur ou pharmacien (pharmacienne)? Donnez vos raisons.

Imaginons et discutons!

In the illustration on the preceding page, each of the five persons is in the drugstore for a different reason. A few minutes later they are all talking to one another.

Enact their conversation in French.

to drive, steer **conduire**
to park **garer**
to blow a horn **klaxonner**
to sit down **s'asseoir**
to be seated **être assis(e)**
to be equipped with **être équipé(e)
   de**
to put into (first gear) **mettre en
   (première)**
to hang **être accroché(e)**
to work *(function)* **marcher, aller**
to rain **pleuvoir**
to snow **neiger**
to show, portray **représenter**
to pay attention (to) **faire attention
   (à)**

in good condition **en bon état**
in order to **de façon à**
economical **économique**
a great deal of, a lot of **pas mal de**
English **anglais**
roomy **spacieux (spacieuse)**
responsive *(of motors)* **nerveux
   (nerveuse)**

car **la voiture**
used car **la voiture d'occasion**
driver **le (la) conducteur
   (conductrice)**
engine **le moteur**
interior **l'intérieur** *(m.)*
front seat **le siège avant**
rear seat **le siège arrière**
seat belt **la ceinture de sécurité**
steering wheel **le volant**
horn **le klaxon**
hood **le capot**
windshield **le pare-brise**
windshield wiper **l'essuie-glace** *(m.)*
model **le modèle**
new model **un modèle récent**
part **la pièce**
glove compartment **la boîte à gants**
dashboard **le tableau de bord**
clock **la pendule**
radio **la radio**
button, knob **le bouton**
stickshift **le levier de vitesse**

heater **le chauffage**
air conditioning **la climatisation**
speed **la vitesse**
speedometer **l'indicateur** *(m.)* **de
   vitesse**
odometer, mileage gauge
   le compteur kilométrique
gear *(first, second, etc.)* **la vitesse**
clutch pedal **la pédale d'embrayage**
   (m.)
accelerator **l'accélérateur** *(m.)*
brake pedal **la pédale de frein**
emergency brake **le frein à main**
power brake **le frein moteur**
bucket seat **le siège baquet**
light **la lumière**
door **la portière**
handle **la poignée**
window *(of a vehicle)* **la glace**
electric windows **les glaces
   automatiques**
side mirror **le rétroviseur extérieur**
rear-view mirror **le rétroviseur**

sun visor **le pare-soleil** *(same pl.)*
armrest **l'accoudoir** *(m.)*
ash tray **le cendrier**
automatic transmission
   **le changement de vitesse
   automatique**
standard (stick) transmission
   **le changement de vitesse
   manuel**
miles per hour **miles** *(m.)* **à l'heure**
kilometers per hour **kilomètres** *(m.)*
   à l'heure
second **la seconde**
market **le marché**
luxury **le luxe**

La voiture

Analyse de l'illustration

1. Cette voiture est-elle équipée de glaces automatiques? Comment le savez-vous?
2. Comment savons-nous que cette voiture n'est pas un modèle anglais?
3. Qu'est-ce qu'il y a entre les pare-soleil?
4. Que voit-on sur le tableau de bord?
5. Que vous indique le levier de vitesse?
6. Combien de pédales y a-t-il dans une voiture à changement de vitesse automatique? Quelles sont-elles?
7. À quoi sert la boîte à gants?
8. Où se trouve la ceinture de sécurité?
9. Comment savez-vous que cette voiture a un siège arrière?
10. Qu'est-ce qu'il y a sur la portière droite que l'on ne peùt pas voir sur la portière gauche?
11. Où devrions-nous être assis de façon à voir le dessin tel qu'il est représenté?
12. Où est le moteur?
13. À quoi sert le klaxon?

Points de départ

14. Quelle est la différence entre un compteur kilométrique et un indicateur de vitesse?
15. Quand a-t-on besoin du frein à main?
16. Si vous conduisez à 100 km à l'heure, quelle est votre vitesse en miles à l'heure?
17. Si vous avez fait 800 miles en voiture, combien de kilomètres avez-vous faits?
18. Quelle est l'utilité des rétroviseurs?
19. Quand se sert-on des essuie-glaces?
20. Décrivez votre voiture ou celle que vous aimeriez avoir.

Sujets de discussion

1. Description de l'intérieur d'une voiture.
2. Comment choisir une automobile.
3. Un bon chauffeur doit faire attention à pas mal de choses.

Imaginons et discutons!

Imagine that you meet with the last four owners of your used car. What do they say about its present condition? Why did each of them buy or sell it? In retrospect, were their decisions wise ones?

Enact the dialog in French.

to fill **remplir**
to fill the gas tank **faire le plein**
to get *(water, gas)* **prendre**
to lubricate, grease **graisser**
to change oil **changer l'huile**
to turn on *(headlights)* **allumer**
to run *(of an engine)* **être en marche, tourner**
to charge *(battery)* **charger**
to discharge *(battery)* **décharger**
to save (on) **faire des économies (de)**
to drive *(a vehicle)* **conduire**
to drive (to) **aller (à)**
to drive *(intr.)* **rouler**
to own **avoir, posséder**
to damage, do harm to **abîmer, endommager**
to take a trip **faire un voyage**
to use up, consume **consommer**
"to kill two birds with one stone" **‹faire d'une pierre deux coups›**
to owe **devoir**
to check, examine **vérifier**

foreign **étranger (étrangère)**
elsewhere **autre part, ailleurs**
slowly **lentement**
roomy **spacieux (spacieuse)**
dependable **fiable**
responsive *(of motors)* **nerveux (nerveuse)**

service station **la station-service**
gas pump **la pompe à essence**
automobile, car **la voiture**
convertible **la décapotable**
sports car **la voiture de sport**
station wagon **le break**
motorist, driver **l'automobiliste** *(m., f.)*, **le (la) conducteur (conductrice)**
tire **le pneu**
spare tire **la roue de secours, le pneu de rechange**
wheel **la roue**
trunk **le coffre**
headlight **le phare**
tail light **le feu arrière**
parking light **le feu de position**
bumper **le pare-chocs**
tank **le réservoir**
rack **la plate-forme élévatrice**
license plate **la plaque d'immatriculation** *(f.)*

driver's license **le permis de conduire**
battery **la batterie**
radiator **le radiateur**
crankcase **le carter**
seat **le siège**
service **le service**
attendant **l'employé(e)**
mechanic **le (la) mécanicien (mécanicienne)**
self-service **le self-service**
hose **le tuyau**
water **l'eau** *(f.)*
air pressure **la pression**
gasoline **l'essence** *(f.)*
gallon **le gallon** *(3.7 litres)*
liter **le litre** *(0.26 gallons)*
oil **l'huile** *(f.)*
lubrication **le graissage**
oil filter **le filtre à l'huile**
expense(s) **les frais** *(m. pl.)*
map **la carte**

À la station-service

23

Analyse de l'illustration

1. Que fait le conducteur de la voiture?
2. Qu'est-ce qui nous fait penser qu'il se prépare à faire un voyage?
3. Que fait l'employé au premier plan?
4. Quelles parties de la voiture pouvez-vous voir?
5. Où se trouve la deuxième voiture? Pourquoi?
6. Quelle différence y a-t-il entre les deux voitures?
7. Pourquoi est-ce que le mécanicien est en train de «faire d'une pierre deux coups»?
8. Qu'est-ce qui vous fait penser que la voiture sur le dessin est une voiture étrangère?

Points de départ

9. À quoi sert la plaque d'immatriculation? Pourquoi a-t-on besoin d'un permis de conduire?
10. Quand faites-vous mettre de l'eau dans votre radiateur?
11. Si l'essence coûte 2,00 dollars le gallon, combien dépenserez-vous pour remplir un réservoir de 15 gallons?
12. Si vous remplissez votre réservoir avec soixante litres d'essence, combien de gallons avez-vous achetés?
13. Après combien de miles changez-vous l'huile dans le carter en général?
14. Quels services pouvez-vous obtenir dans une station-service?
15. Expliquez le terme "self-service".
16. Pourquoi ne doit-on pas allumer les phares si le moteur n'est pas en marche?
17. Pourquoi est-il difficile de graisser une voiture ailleurs que dans une station-service ou un garage?
18. Décrivez votre voiture ou celle de vos parents.
19. À dix-huit miles au gallon, combien de miles pouvez-vous faire avec vingt gallons d'essence dans votre réservoir?
20. Pourquoi la plupart des garages ont-ils plusieurs pompes à essence?

Sujets de discussion

1. Les frais d'une voiture.
2. Le travail d'un(e) employé(e) de station-service.
3. Comment faire des économies d'essence.

Imaginons et discutons!

Imagine that the man holding a map in the illustration on the preceding page is going on a long journey. The mechanic notices that his car is not in very good condition and tells him that a few things need to be fixed before he leaves. The man is very thankful for his advice but has some concerns.

Enact the dialog in French.

to take off **décoller**
to land **atterrir**
to fasten the seat belt **attacher la ceinture de sécurité**
to smoke **fumer**
to wave **faire signe (de la main)**
to check baggage **(faire) enregistrer les bagages**
to pick up baggage **aller chercher, récupérer les bagages**
to declare, pay duty on **déclarer à la douane**
to inspect **fouiller**
to lose **perdre**
to be about to **se préparer à**
to have just (+ *past part.*) **venir de (+ *inf.*)**
to show **présenter, montrer**
to talk to one another **se parler**
to occupy **occuper**
to make a reservation **faire une réservation**
to board (a plane) **monter à bord, embarquer**
to go by plane **aller en avion**
to travel **voyager**

from **de**
to **à**
during **pendant**
forbidden **défendu(e)**
duty-free **en franchise**
panic stricken **affolé(e)**
calm **calme**

airport **l'aéroport** (*m.*)
airline **la compagnie (ligne) aérienne**
airplane **l'avion** (*m.*)
jet **le jet**
pilot **le pilote**
flight attendant **l'hôtesse** (*f.*) **de l'air**
steward (*m.*) **le steward**
passenger **le (la) passager (passagère)**
tourist **le (la) touriste**
flight **le vol**
flight to... **le vol à destination de...**
take off **le décollage**
landing **l'atterrissage** (*m.*)
runway **la piste**
engine **le réacteur**
propeller **l'hélice** (*f.*)
cockpit **la cabine de pilotage**
wing **l'aile** (*f.*)
tail **la queue**
function **la fonction**
seat **le siège**

first class **la première classe**
economy class **la classe touriste**
front seat **le siège avant**
waiting list **la liste d'attente**
shop, store **le magasin**
goods **la marchandise**
service, duty **le service**
ticket **le billet, le ticket**
ticket office **le guichet**
travel agency **l'agence** (*f.*) **de voyages**
(*travel*) route **l'itinéraire** (*m.*)
reservation **la réservation**
gate **la porte**
observation platform **la terrasse d'observation** (*f.*)
control tower **la tour de contrôle**
waiting room **la salle d'attente**
customs **la douane**
customs officer **le (la) douanier (douanière)**
immigration **l'immigration** (*f.*)
documents **les papiers** (*m. pl.*)

passport **le passeport**
baggage inspection **l'inspection** (*f.*) **des bagages** (*m. pl.*)
baggage-claim room **la consigne**
list **la liste**
baby **le bébé**
difficulty **le problème**
cart **le chariot**
flag **le drapeau**
person taking part (in) **le (la) participant(e) (à)**

À l'aéroport

24

Analyse de l'illustration

1. Pourquoi l'avion à l'arrière plan n'a-t-il pas d'hélices?
2. Regardez le drapeau sur la queue de l'avion. De quelle compagnie aérienne peut-il s'agir?
3. Où sont les pilotes des deux avions?
4. Où se trouve l'hôtesse de l'air?
5. Comment savez-vous que l'avion au premier plan se prépare à partir?
6. Qui pourrait avoir des ennuis pendant le vol? Pourquoi?
7. Qui n'a pas fait enregistrer sa petite valise?
8. Que fait le douanier à gauche?
9. Combien de passagers se préparent à embarquer?
10. Où se trouve la salle d'attente?

Points de départ

11. Expliquez ce qu'est une liste d'attente.
12. D'où peut-on faire signe de la main à un(e) passager (passagère)?
13. Que doivent faire les passagers d'un avion au moment du décollage et de l'atterrissage?
14. Quelles sont les différences entre la première classe et la classe touriste?
15. Que se passe-t-il à la douane?
16. Après un vol New York-Paris, où devez-vous présenter vos papiers après être allé(e) chercher vos bagages?
17. Qu'est-ce qu'un touriste?
18. Décrivez les services d'une agence de voyages.
19. Pourquoi n'y a-t-il pas de bureaux de douane dans un aéroport où il n'y a que des vols intérieurs?
20. Qu'est-ce qu'une marchandise en franchise?

Sujets de discussion

1. Description d'un aéroport.
2. Quand la ligne aérienne a perdu mes valises.
3. Les responsabilités d'un steward ou d'une hôtesse de l'air.

Imaginons et discutons!

An international flight has covered most of the distance to Paris. Some passengers are walking about and conversing, since it has been a long flight.

Enact the discussion among several passengers in French.

to travel **voyager**
to depart **partir**
to arrive **arriver**
to catch *(a train)* **attraper**
to take **prendre**
to stop (at) **s'arrêter (à)**
to carry **porter**
to check baggage **faire enregistrer
ses bagages**
to browse, leaf through **feuilleter,
parcourir**
to help **aider**
to replace **remplacer**
to be late **être en retard**
to claim baggage **aller chercher,
récupérer ses bagages**
to change *(train)* **changer de**
to happen, go on **se passer**
to meet *(to get to know)* **faire la
connaissance de, rencontrer**
to check **vérifier**

main **principal(e)**
instead of **au lieu de**
inexpensive **économique, bon
marché**
late **tard**
early **tôt, de bonne heure**
on time **à l'heure**
electric **électrique**
take your seats! **en voiture!**

railroad station **la gare**
ticket **le billet**
ticket window **le guichet**
one-way ticket **le billet simple**
round-trip ticket **le billet d'aller et
retour**
timetable **l'horaire** *(m.)*
time of arrival **l'heure** *(f.)* **d'arrivée**
(f.)
time of departure **l'heure** *(f.)* **de
départ** *(m)*
train **le train**
freight train **le train de
marchandises**
express train **l'express** *(m.)*
local train **l'omnibus** *(m.)*
locomotive **la locomotive**
conductor **le (la) contrôleur
(contrôleuse)**
engineer **le (la) mécanicien
(mécanicienne)**
porter **le (la) porteur (porteuse)**
baggage check room **la consigne**

locker **la consigne automatique**
suitcase **la valise**
baggage **les bagages** *(m. pl.)*
passenger **le (la) passager
(passagère)**
first class **la première classe**
second class **la seconde classe**
waiting room **la salle d'attente**
pullman **le wagon-lit**
diner, dining car
le wagon-restaurant
vehicle, car, carriage **le wagon**
track **la voie ferrée**
cart **le chariot**
newstand **le kiosque à journaux**
magazine **la revue, le magazine**
old lady **la vieille dame**
snack bar **le buffet**
overcoat **le pardessus**
time *(clock time)* **l'heure** *(f.)*

À la gare

25

Analyse de l'illustration

1. Quel genre de locomotive voyez-vous sur l'illustration?
2. Où se trouvent le mécanicien et les conducteurs?
3. Que fait le jeune homme devant le kiosque à journaux?
4. À qui appartiennent les valises sur le chariot?
5. Que se passe-t-il au guichet?
6. Que fait le monsieur qui a son pardessus sur le bras?
7. Décrivez tout ce que vous voyez sur le dessin.

Points de départ

8. Que font les contrôleurs dans un train?
9. Que signifie l'expression «en voiture!»?
10. Comment un(e) porteur (porteuse) peut-il (elle) vous aider?
11. Combien donnez-vous au (à la) porteur (porteuse) qui a apporté vos quatre valises au train?
12. Que peut-on faire dans une gare s'il faut attendre le train pendant longtemps?
13. Où peut-on manger dans un train?
14. Quel est l'avantage d'un billet d'aller et retour sur un billet simple?
15. Pourquoi est-ce qu'un train de marchandises n'a pas de wagons-lit?
16. Qu'est-ce qu'un horaire?
17. Où peut-on déposer ses bagages si l'on arrive à la gare de bonne heure?
18. Quel autre endroit y a-t-il pour déposer ses bagages à la gare?
19. Quelle est la différence la plus importante entre un express et un omnibus?
20. Si un train arrive à 11 heures et repart à 14 heures, combien de temps sera-t-il resté en gare?

Sujets de discussion

1. Racontez la vie d'un(e) porteur (porteuse).
2. Avantages et inconvénients des voyages en train.
3. Les trains européens comparés aux trains américains.

Imaginons et discutons!

In the railroad station of Mâcon, halfway to Marseille, passengers on the Paris-Marseille express were allowed to leave the train for a few minutes. Two of them missed the "All aboard" and the train left, along with their baggage. Imagine you are one of these passengers and must solve the problems, beginning at the ticket window.

Enact the situation in the railroad station in French.

to take a trip **faire un voyage**
to take a cruise **faire une croisière**
to travel **voyager**
to visit (a place) **visiter**
to go sailing, to sail *(for a person)*
    faire de la voile
to sail *(for a ship)* **partir**
to be seasick **avoir le mal de mer**
to sink **couler**
to wave (one's hand) **faire signe (de
    la main)**
to stroll **flâner**

responsible **responsable**
together **ensemble**
ready **prêt(e)**
according to **d'après**
doubtless **sans doute**
in port **à quai**
rough **agité(e)**
smooth **calme**

harbor, port **le port**
pier, deck **le quai**
ship **le bateau, le navire**
cruise ship **le bateau de croisière**
captain **le capitaine** (*no fem.:* **elle
    est capitaine**)
sailor **le matelot, le marin** (*no
    fem.:* **elle est matelot ou marin**)
uniform **l'uniforme** *(m.)*
passenger **le (la) passager
    (passagère)**
lifeboat **le canot de sauvetage**
tugboat **le remorqueur**
freighter **le cargo**
liner **le paquebot**
submarine **le sous-marin**
aircraft carrier **le porte-avion**
destroyer **le contre-torpilleur**
navy **la marine**
deck **le pont**
porthole **le hublot**
mast **le mât**
pennant **le drapeau, le pavillon**

propeller **l'hélice** *(f.)*
side **le côté**
bow **la proue, l'avant** *(m.)*
stern **la poupe, l'arrière** *(m.)*
starboard **le tribord**
port *(left)* **bâbord**
end, extremity **le bout, l'extrémité**
    (f.)
cabin **la cabine**
sea **la mer**
skyline **la ligne d'horizon**
smoke **la fumée**
smokestack **la cheminée**
seagull **la mouette**
truck **le camion**
building **le bâtiment**

Au port

26

Analyse de l'illustration

1. D'où vient la fumée?
2. Où voyez-vous un camion?
3. Décrivez la ligne d'horizon sur le dessin.
4. Où voyez-vous des drapeaux sur le dessin?
5. Comment savez-vous que la dame au premier plan, à gauche, connaît quelqu'un sur le paquebot?
6. Décrivez le port.
7. Combien de ponts peut-on voir? Qui est sur les ponts?
8. Où sont les hublots?
9. Pourquoi y a-t-il presque toujours des mouettes dans un port?
10. De quoi peuvent parler les trois hommes qui sont ensemble sur le quai?
11. D'après le dessin, pouvez-vous dire ce qui est l'avant et ce qui est l'arrière du paquebot? Expliquez pourquoi.
12. Qu'est-ce qui vous fait penser que le gros bateau à l'arrière-plan du dessin est sans doute un cargo?
13. Pourquoi ne peut-on voir aucune cabine?
14. Comment savez-vous que le paquebot à quai n'est pas un bateau de la marine?

Points de départ

15. Qui est responsable de tout ce qui se passe sur un paquebot?
16. Quand se sert-on des canots de sauvetage?
17. À quelle extrémité d'un bateau l'hélice se trouve-t-elle?
18. Si quelqu'un vous offrait un voyage en France aimeriez-vous y aller (si non, pourquoi?), et quand seriez-vous prêt(e) à partir?
19. Qu'est-ce qu'un sous-marin?
20. Quelles sont les différences entre un navire de la marine et un bateau de croisière?

Sujets de discussion

1. La mer.
2. Le voyage que j'aimerais faire (ou que j'ai déjà fait).
3. Un port vu du pont d'un bateau.

★ ★
Imaginons et discutons!

★

This is your first cruise. As the ship leaves the dock, you stroll on the decks and discuss what you see with other passengers more knowledgeable than you about ships and the routine of the sea.

Enact this dialog in French.

to post *(a letter)* **poster**
to mail **envoyer**
to deliver **livrer, remettre**
to register a letter **envoyer une
lettre en recommandé**
to weigh **peser**
to hold **tenir**
to lose **perdre**
to look for **chercher**
to stamp **timbrer**
to pull out, take out **tirer**
to indicate **indiquer**

to the left **de gauche, à gauche**
high *(of prices)* **élevé(e), cher
(chère)**
mail, postal **postal(e)**
blue **bleu(e)**
red **rouge**
by airmail **par avion**
C.O.D. **livrable contre
remboursement, payable à
l'arrivée**

postal system **le système postal**
post office **la poste**
(clerk's) window **le guichet**
letter carrier **le facteur** *(no fem.:*
elle est facteur)
letter **la lettre**
postcard **la carte postale**
telegram **le télégramme**
parcel post **le colis postal**
envelope **l'enveloppe** *(f.)*
mail **le courrier**
mailbox **la boîte aux lettres**
post-office box **la boîte postale**
letter slot **la fente de la boîte aux
lettres**
general delivery **poste restante**
mail delivery **la distribution du
courrier**
home delivery **la distribution à
domicile**
special delivery **la distribution
exprès**

special delivery stamp **le timbre
exprès**
regular mail *(first class)* **le courrier
régulier**
second-class mail **l'imprimé** *(m.)*
registered letter **la lettre
recommandée**
postage **l'affranchissement**
domestic postage **le tarif postal
intérieur**
foreign postage **l'affranchissement
pour l'étranger** *(m.)*
stamp **le timbre**
book of stamps **un carnet de
timbres**
commemorative stamp **le timbre
commémoratif**
rate **le tarif**
postmark **le cachet de la poste**
the date **la date**
return address **l'adresse** *(f.)* **de
l'expéditeur** *(m.)*

package **le paquet**
ounce *(28.4 grams)* **l'once** *(f.)*
pound *(.45 kilogram)* **la livre**
ZIP code **le code postal**
United States **les États-Unis**
purse **le porte-monnaie**
color **la couleur**
day **le jour, la journée**
week **la semaine**

À la poste

27

Analyse de l'illustration

1. Que fait la dame au premier plan avec les deux mains?
2. Comment savons-nous que cette dame aura bientôt besoin de timbres?
3. Que fait la dame à gauche?
4. Qui porte des paquets?
5. À votre avis que fait l'homme qui porte un chapeau à droite?

Points de depart

6. Quel est le prix d'un timbre pour une lettre (tarif postal intérieur) par courrier régulier?
7. Quel est l'affranchissement d'une carte postale aux États-Unis?
8. Que veut dire «livrable contre remboursement»?
9. Comment savez-vous qu'une enveloppe va être envoyée «par avion»?
10. Quelles sont les différentes actions que vous faites quand vous voulez envoyer une lettre par la poste?
11. Pourquoi le tarif d'affranchissement pour l'étranger est-il plus élevé que pour les États-Unis?
12. Quel est le jour de la semaine où il n'y a pas de distribution de courrier aux États-Unis?
13. Pourquoi une lettre est-elle envoyée «poste restante»?
14. En général, que vous indique le cachet de la poste?
15. Combien de grammes y a-t-il dans deux onces?
16. Quelle est la différence entre le courrier régulier et une lettre recommandée?
17. Où doit-on mettre l'adresse de l'expéditeur sur une enveloppe aux États-Unis?
18. Quand envoie-t-on une lettre en recommandé?
19. Que se passe-t-il si vous envoyez une lettre non timbrée?
20. Pourquoi devez-vous peser un paquet avant de l'envoyer?

Sujets de discussion

1. La journée d'un facteur.
2. Un télégramme.
3. Le système postal des États-Unis.

Imaginons et discutons!

While waiting in line at the post office, customers exchange information and express their opinions on the postal system. As the line moves forward, each makes a different purchase or request at the clerk's window.

Enact the dialog among customers and with the clerk in French.

to register **s'inscrire; signer le registre**
to reserve **réserver**
to welcome **accueillir**
to check into a hotel **arriver à l'hôtel**
to check out of a hotel **quitter l'hôtel**
to stay at a hotel **descendre à l'hôtel, séjourner dans un hôtel**
to carry **porter**
to show to one's room **conduire à sa chambre**
to pay the bill **payer la note**
to clean the room **nettoyer la chambre**
to call **faire venir, appeler**
to ask **demander**
to contain **contenir**
to be supposed to **devoir**
to receive, get **recevoir**
to bring bad luck **porter malheur**

satisfied **satisfait(e)**
dissatisfied **mécontent(e)**
unlucky **fatidique, qui porte malheur**
outside (of) **en dehors de**
at your service **à votre service**
(facing) the backyard **(sur) la cour**
first class **de première classe**
confusing **déroutante**

hotel **l'hôtel** (*m.*)
motel **le motel**
front desk **la réception**
desk clerk **le (la) réceptionniste**
doorman **le (la) portier (portière)**
bellhop **le groom** (*no fem.:* **elle est groom**)
(*hotel*) guest **le (la) client(e)**
suitcase, bag **la valise**
hotel manager **le (la) directeur (directrice) de l'hôtel**
luggage, bags **les bagages** (*m. pl.*)
lobby **le hall**
elevator **l'ascenseur** (*m.*)
rug **le tapis**
mirror **le miroir**
floor (*on which one walks*) **le plancher**
floor (*unit of counting*) **l'étage** (*m.*)
first floor (*European ground floor*) **le rez-de-chaussée**
second floor (*European first floor*) **le premier étage**

key **la clef**
mail **le courrier**
set of mailboxes; pigeonholes **les cases** (*f. pl.*) **à courrier**
(*married*) couple **le couple**
chambermaid **la femme de chambre**
service **le service**
room service **être servi dans sa chambre**
valet **le valet de chambre**
tip **le pourboire, le service**
fur coat **le manteau de fourrure**
hat **le chapeau**
handbag **le sac à main**
arm **le bras**
superstition **la superstition**
noise **le bruit**
traveler **le (la) voyageur (voyageuse)**
street **la rue**

À l'hôtel

28

1. Qu'est-ce qui vous fait penser que l'hôtel sur le dessin est un hôtel de première classe?
2. Qui porte un chapeau?
3. Combien de valises voyez-vous et où sont-elles?
4. Combien d'ascenseurs y a-t-il et où sont-ils?
5. Comment savons-nous que le couple au premier plan vient d'arriver à l'hôtel?
6. Décrivez la jeune femme au premier plan.
7. Qui donne une clef à qui, et pourquoi?
8. Où sont les cases à courrier et que contiennent-elles?
9. Que voyez-vous à droite, à l'arrière-plan?
10. Combien de grooms pouvez-vous voir? Où sont-ils? Que font-ils?

Points de départ

11. Dans un hôtel, quand le (la) client (cliente) doit-il (elle) payer sa note?
12. Quand et pourquoi donne-t-on, en général, un pourboire au groom?
13. Quand et pourquoi une personne demande-t-elle à être servie dans sa chambre?
14. Savez-vous que la plupart des grands hôtels n'ont pas de treizième étage? Quelle en est la raison?
15. Savez-vous qu'en dehors des États-Unis ce que nous appelons le premier étage est le rez-de-chaussée, ce que nous appelons le second étage est le premier étage, etc.? Que pensez-vous de cette différence?
16. Pourquoi est-ce que la plupart des motels n'ont pas d'ascenseurs?
17. En général, qui nettoie les chambres dans un hôtel, quand et combien de fois?
18. Quand vous êtes à l'hôtel, préférez-vous une chambre sur la cour ou une chambre sur la rue? Pourquoi?
19. Préférez-vous séjourner dans des hôtels ou dans des motels? Pourquoi?
20. Comment est-ce qu'une personne reçoit son courrier à l'hôtel?

Sujets de discussion

1. Les différences entre un hôtel et un motel typiques.
2. Le travail d'un(e) réceptionniste dans un hôtel.
3. Ce qu'un groom m'a dit.

★ ★

Imaginons et discutons!

★

While a bellhop waits with their bags, a family of four is about to check in at the front desk of a large hotel where they had reserved two double rooms for three nights. Enact in French the scenes that get them registered, then transported to their floor, and finally installed in their designated rooms.

Carte

RESTAURANT de PARIS

HORS D'ŒUVRES (APPETIZERS)	Prix
Hors d'oeuvres variés	45 F.
Assiette de fruits de mer (shellfish platter)	60
Pâté maison	35
Salade de tomates (tomato salad)	30
Caviar Russe (Russian caviar)	130

LES SOUPES (SOUPS)

Crème d'asperges (asparagus soup)	28
Soupe de poisson (fish soup)	32
Crème de champignons (mushroom soup)	28
Soupe à l'oignon (onion soup)	32
Bouillabaisse (seafood stew)	140

LES ŒUFS (EGGS)

Œufs au plat (fried eggs)	25
Œufs brouillés au jambon (scrambled eggs with ham)	30
Œufs brouillés aux champignons (scrambled eggs with mushrooms)	28
Omelette de campagne (omelette, country style)	28
Omelette aux fines herbes (omelette with herbs)	28

LES LÉGUMES (VEGETABLES)

Épinard à la crème (creamed spinach)	28
Cœurs d'artichauts au jambon (artichokes with diced ham)	35
Haricots verts (green beans)	28
Poivrons farcis (stuffed peppers)	40
Aubergines (eggplant)	32
Petits pois (peas)	30

LES VIANDES (MEATS) F

Filet grillé (grilled filet mignon)	
Châteaubriand, pour 2 personnes (sliced filet, for 2)	
Poulet rôti (roast chicken)	
Canard à l'orange (duck with orange sauce)	
Côtelettes de veau (veal chops)	
Côtelettes de mouton (lamb chops)	
Rognons de veau au Madère (kidney cooked in Madeira)	
Rôti de bœuf (roast beef)	
Entrecôte de Paris	

DESSERTS ET FROMAGES (DESSERTS AND CHEESES)

Crème au caramel (custard with caramel sauce)	
Tarte aux fraises (strawberry tart)	
Macédoine de fruits (fruit cocktail)	
Fruits frais variés (selection of fresh fruits)	
Glaces diverses (various flavors of ice cream)	
Fromages variés (selection of cheeses)	

BOISSONS (BEVERAGES)

Vins rouges (red wines)	40
Vins blancs (white wines)	40
Vins rosés (rosé wines)	40
Champagnes (champagne)	140-
Bières (beer)	15
Eaux minérales (bottled water)	
Perrier (bottled water, carbonated)	
Boissons gazeuses (soft drinks)	
Limonade (lemon soda)	
Thé (tea)	
Café (coffee)	
Liqueurs, cognacs, whiskys	

Service obligatoire 15% (15% service charge)

---

to choose **choisir**
to have (eat, drink) **prendre**
to serve **servir**
to ask for, request, order **commander**
to try (out), test, sample **goûter**
to be sold out, be out of **ne plus en avoir**
to put on the bill **ajouter à l'addition**
to leave a tip **laisser un pourboire**
to cost **coûter**
to prepare, fix **préparer**
to be full **être rassasié(e)**
to remember **se souvenir**
to bring **apporter**
to go off **s'éloigner**
to split **partager**

expensive **cher (chère)**
inexpensive **bon marché**
complete, full **complet (complète)**
fresh **frais (fraîche)**
canned **en boîte**
well done **bien cuit(e)**
medium **à point**
rare **saignant(e)**
medium (price) **moyen**
on an average **en moyenne**
both **les deux**
how much is...? **combien coûte...?**
instead of **au lieu de**
in the course of **au cours de**
approximately **à peu près**
imaginary **imaginaire**
special **spécial(e)**
as much as **autant**
delicious **délicieux (délicieuse)**
appealing **tentant(e)**

meal **le repas**
menu **le menu**
dish, course (of a meal) **le plat**
seafood **les fruits de mer** (shrimps, crabs, etc.) ; **les poissons** (fish)
waiter **le garçon**
waitress **la serveuse**
service **le service**
bill, check **l'addition** (f.) , **la note**
tip **le pourboire**
mistake **l'erreur** (f.)
complaint **la réclamation**
dollar **le dollar**
monetary unit of France **le franc** (abbrev.: **F**) ($1 = à peu près 6 francs)
United States **les États-Unis**
category **la catégorie**

Analyse de l'illustration

1. Nommez deux plats qu'on sert rarement dans les restaurants aux États-Unis.
2. Nommez deux plats qui sont très populaires aux États-Unis.
3. Nommez deux plats que vous n'avez jamais goûtés.
4. Quel est le plat le plus cher de la carte?
5. Quels sont les fruits de mer et les poissons que vous voyez sur la carte?
6. De tous les desserts, lequel vous semble le plus tentant? Pourquoi?
7. Quel est le dessert le moins cher?
8. En prenant la carte, commandez un repas complet à un garçon imaginaire.
9. Dans quelle catégorie se trouve ce restaurant—cher, bon marché ou moyen—d'après les prix de la carte?

Points de départ

10. En France on mange généralement «à la carte» ou on choisit un menu. Expliquez la différence.
11. Comment aimez-vous le filet?
12. Si vous commandez un menu qui coûte 100F., quel pourboire sera ajouté à l'addition?
13. Quel est le prix, en dollars, d'un menu qui vous a coûté 135F.?
14. Si les Français ne prennent pas de café au cours de leurs repas, quand le prennent-ils?
15. Quelle boisson préférez-vous avec votre repas?
16. Quel vin préférez-vous avec la viande? Et avec le poisson?
17. Quelle boisson préférez-vous avec un bon fromage? Que préférez-vous ne pas boire avec votre fromage?
18. En francs français, combien coûtent, en moyenne, deux œufs au plat dans un restaurant bon marché aux États-Unis? Et une glace au chocolat pour une personne?
19. Vous aviez commandé des côtelettes de mouton, mais le garçon vous informe qu'il n'y en a plus. Que faites-vous?
20. Que faites-vous s'il y a une erreur dans l'addition?

Sujets de discussion

1. Expliquez la différence entre un repas typiquement français et un repas typiquement américain.
2. Le repas que je ferais si les prix n'avaient pas d'importance.
3. Un plat spécial que je sais préparer.

★ ★

Imaginons et discutons!

★

After enjoying a leisurely meal at the Restaurant de Paris in the city of the same name, a group of friends has a few problems to solve before leaving: 1) some of the charges on the bill seem incorrect; 2) who will pay the bill?; 3) who will leave the tip and how much?

Enact the situation in French.

to spend *(money)* **dépenser**
to save **économiser, mettre de côté;**
  épargner
to make payment **payer**
to maintain, keep **maintenir, garder**
to review, go over **revoir, examiner**
to devise, invent **inventer**
to predict **prédire, prévoir**
to amount to **se monter à**
to exceed **dépasser, excéder**
to suggest **proposer**
to be in the course of *(+ gerund)*
  être en train de *(+ inf.)*
to balance (a budget) **équilibrer (un**
  budget)
to happen **arriver, se passer**

medical **médical(e)**
unpredictable **imprévisible**
dental **dentaire**
weekly **hebdomadaire, par semaine**
monthly **mensuel (mensuelle)**
personal **personnel (personnelle)**
high *(of prices)* **élevé(e)**
young **jeune**
if so **si c'est le cas**
if not **dans le cas contraire, sinon**
how much? **combien?**
plus **plus**
minus **moins**
within, inside, in **à l'intérieur, dans**
each, every **chaque, chacun**
  (chacune)

(family) budget **le budget (familial)**
income **le revenu**
expenditure **les frais** *(m. pl.)* ,
  les dépenses *(f. pl.)*
expense **la dépense**
money **l'argent** *(m.)*
payment **le paiement**
down payment **l'acompte** *(m.)* ,
  les arrhes *(f. pl.)*
purchase **l'achat** *(m.)*
installment purchase **l'achat à**
  tempérament
amount **le total, la somme totale**
bill **la facture**
salary **le salaire**
dollar **le dollar**
checkbook **le carnet de chèques**
bank **la banque**
credit card **la carte de crédit**
checking account **le compte courant**
banknote **le billet de banque**
electronic calculator **la calculatrice**
cost of living **le coût de la vie**

rent **le loyer**
mortgage **l'hypothèque** *(f.)*
utilities **les services publics**
tax, taxes **l'impôt** *(m.)* , **la taxe**
insurance **l'assurance** *(f.)*
interest **l'intérêt** *(m.)*
transportation **le transport**
clothes, clothing **les habits,**
  les vêtements
food, groceries **la nourriture,**
  l'alimentation *(f.)*
entertainment **le divertissement,**
  la distraction
vacation **les vacances** *(f. pl.)*
pocket money, spending money,
  allowance **l'argent** *(m.)* **de poche**
year **l'année** *(f.)*
husband **le mari, l'époux**
wife **la femme, l'épouse**
(married) couple **le couple,**
  le ménage
child **l'enfant** *(m.)*
baby **le bébé**

crib **le berceau**
bedroom **la chambre à coucher**
table **la table**
lamp **la lampe**
ballpoint pen **le stylo**
sheet of paper **la feuille de papier**
envelope **l'enveloppe** *(f.)*
solution **la solution**

Le budget familial

Analyse de l'illustration

1. Que voyez-vous dans la chambre à coucher?
2. Comment sait-on que la scène se passe le soir?
3. Nommez les objets qui sont sur la table.
4. Que pensez-vous que le mari dise à sa femme?
5. Que pensez-vous que la femme dise à son mari?
6. Quel pourrait être le principal problème du couple en train d'examiner ses dépenses familiales?
7. Pourquoi ce ménage doit-il avoir un budget?
8. Si ce couple n'a qu'un enfant, à combien se montent les dépenses de nourriture par semaine à votre avis?
9. Inventez le budget mensuel de ce couple.

Points de départ

10. Qu'est-ce qu'un budget?
11. Quel est l'avantage de faire un budget?
12. Avez-vous un budget pour vos frais personnels? Si c'est le cas, pourquoi? Sinon, pourquoi n'en avez-vous pas?
13. Quelle est votre dépense mensuelle la plus élevée?
14. Si vos frais dépassent vos revenus, quelles sont les solutions que vous proposez?
15. Si vous économisez $10 par semaine pendant cinq ans, combien d'argent (plus les intérêts) aurez-vous en banque?
16. Enumérez quelques frais typiques nécessaires dans le budget mensuel d'un jeune ménage.
17. On ne peut pas prévoir toutes les dépenses. Nommez quelques frais totalement imprévisibles.
18. Expliquez ce qu'est un achat à tempérament.
19. Quels sont les avantages et les inconvénients d'une carte de crédit?
20. Qu'est-ce que l'argent de poche?

Sujets de discussion

1. Mon budget.
2. Comment économiser de l'argent.
3. Le couple et son nouveau bébé.

★ ★

Imaginons et discutons!

★

Three people are comparing their monthly expenditures. One exceeds his/her budget almost every month and never has enough money. Another is able to save money every month. The expenses of the third can never be predicted.

Enact this discussion in French, including each person's explanation of his/her situation and any plans he/she has to change it.

1992

	D L M M J V S	D L M M J V S	D L M M J V S	D L M M J V S

Janvier
1 2 3 4
5 6 7 8 9 10 11
12 13 14 15 16 17 18
19 20 21 22 23 24 25
26 27 28 29 30 31

Février
1
2 3 4 5 6 7 8
9 10 11 12 13 14 15
16 17 18 19 20 21 22
23 24 25 26 27 28 29

Mars
1 2 3 4 5 6 7
8 9 10 11 12 13 14
15 16 17 18 19 20 21
22 23 24 25 26 27 28
29 30 31

Avril
1 2 3 4
5 6 7 8 9 10 11
12 13 14 15 16 17 18
19 20 21 22 23 24 25
26 27 28 29 30

Mai
1 2
3 4 5 6 7 8 9
10 11 12 13 14 15 16
17 18 19 20 21 22 23
24 25 26 27 28 29 30
31

Juin
1 2 3 4 5 6
7 8 9 10 11 12 13
14 15 16 17 18 19 20
21 22 23 24 25 26 27
28 29 30

Juillet
1 2 3 4
5 6 7 8 9 10 11
12 13 14 15 16 17 18
19 20 21 22 23 24 25
26 27 28 29 30 31

Août
1
2 3 4 5 6 7 8
9 10 11 12 13 14 15
16 17 18 19 20 21 22
23 24 25 26 27 28 29
30 31

Septembre
1 2 3 4 5
6 7 8 9 10 11 12
13 14 15 16 17 18 19
20 21 22 23 24 25 26
27 28 29 30

Octobre
1 2 3
4 5 6 7 8 9 10
11 12 13 14 15 16 17
18 19 20 21 22 23 24
25 26 27 28 29 30 31

Novembre
1 2 3 4 5 6 7
8 9 10 11 12 13 14
15 16 17 18 19 20 21
22 23 24 25 26 27 28
29 30

Décembre
1 2 3 4 5
6 7 8 9 10 11 12
13 14 15 16 17 18 19
20 21 22 23 24 25 26
27 28 29 30 31

---

to occur, fall **avoir lieu, tomber**
to celebrate **célébrer**
to take a long weekend **faire le pont**
to be born **naître, être né(e)**
to consist of **se composer de**
to fall *(night)* **tomber**
to last **durer**
to represent, portray **représenter**

during **durant, pendant**
Catholic **catholique**
the most **le plus (de)**
so that **de sorte que**
early **de bonne heure**
besides **de plus**
as...as **aussi...que**

---

calendar **le calendrier**
date **la date**
month **le mois**
week **la semaine**
Sunday **(le) dimanche**
Monday **(le) lundi**
Tuesday **(le) mardi**
Wednesday **(le) mercredi**
Thursday **(le) jeudi**
Friday **(le) vendredi**
Saturday **(le) samedi**
year **l'année** *(f.)*, **l'an** *(m.)*
leap year **l'année bissextile**
academic year, school year **l'année scolaire**
time **le temps**
hour **l'heure** *(f.)*
minute **la minute**
second **la seconde**
vernal equinox **l'équinoxe** *(m.)* **de printemps**
autumnal equinox **l'équinoxe d'automne**

daylight **la lumière du jour**
standard time **l'heure de Greenwich**
daylight savings time **l'heure d'été**
noon **midi**
midnight **minuit** *(m.)*
workday **le jour de travail, le jour ouvrable**
weekend **le week-end, la fin de la semaine**
long weekend **le pont**
holiday **la fête, le jour férié**
birthday **l'anniversaire** *(m.)* **(de la naissance)**
(wedding) anniversary **l'anniversaire** *(m.)* **(de mariage)**
one's saint's day **sa fête**
Christmas **(le) Noël**
Easter **(les) Pâques** *(m. pl.)*
New Year's Day **le jour de l'An** *(m.)*
eve of **la veille de**
Independence Day **la fête de l'Indépendance**
Labor Day **la fête du Travail**

Memorial Day **la fête du Souvenir**
spring **le printemps**
summer **l'été** *(m.)*
winter **l'hiver** *(m.)*
fall **l'automne** *(m.)*
history **l'histoire** *(f.)*
country **le pays**
United States of America **les États-Unis** *(pl.)*
horoscope **l'horoscope** *(m.)*
characteristic **la caractéristique**
mortal **le mortel**

Le calendrier

Analyse de l'illustration

1. Quels sont les mois qui ont trente et un jours?
2. Quels sont les jours ouvrables de la semaine?
3. Que signifie le mot «week-end»? Que veut dire «faire le pont»?
4. Noël tombera-t-il un lundi en 1992? Quand tombera la fête de l'Indépendance?
5. Quelle sera la date de la fête du Travail en 1992? la fête du Souvenir? la veille du jour de l'An?
6. Quel mois aura un vendredi 13 en 1992?
7. Quels sont les mois qui ont le plus de dimanches sur ce calendrier?

Points de départ

8. Combien de secondes y a-t-il dans une minute? Combien de minutes dans une heure? Combien d'heures dans un jour?
9. Combien de jours y a-t-il dans une semaine? de semaines dans une année? de jours dans une année? de mois dans une année?
10. 1992 sera une année bissextile. Combien d'années bissextiles y a-t-il eu durant votre vie?
11. Quelle est la date de votre anniversaire?
12. Donnez le nom d'une fête française qui n'est pas célébrée aux États-Unis.
13. Qu'est-ce qu'un équinoxe? Pendant quels mois l'équinoxe de printemps et l'équinoxe d'automne ont-ils lieu?
14. Quel est le mois qui a le jour le plus long de l'année, et quel est celui qui a le plus court?
15. Combien d'heures y a-t-il entre midi et minuit?
16. Quel est l'inconvénient de l'heure de Greenwich en été?
17. Nommez trois années importantes dans l'histoire de la France et dites pourquoi elles le sont.
18. Dans les pays catholiques chaque personne célèbre sa fête. Expliquez.
19. Quels sont les mois d'hiver? de printemps? d'été? d'automne?
20. Quel est le personnage dont nous célébrons l'anniversaire partout aux États-Unis? Quel est le jour de sa naissance?

Sujets de discussion

1. Le mois que j'aime le plus.
2. La date la plus importante de l'année scolaire.
3. Mon horoscope.

★ ★

Imaginons et discutons!

Discuss with your classmates aspects of the calendar (such as the length of the work week, seasons, vacations) that you like or dislike. Explain why you feel that way.

Enact the discussion in French.

★

to pay **payer, verser**
to receive **recevoir, percevoir**
to lend **prêter**
to borrow **emprunter**
to deposit **mettre, déposer**
to withdraw **retirer**
to invest **placer; investir**
to open an account **ouvrir un
    compte bancaire**
to cash *(a check)* **toucher**
to fill out *(a form)* **remplir**
to sign **signer**
to get ready (to) **s'apprêter à**
to refer (to) **faire référence à**
to form (start) a line *(of people)* **faire
    la queue**
to work **travailler**
to function, work **fonctionner**
to discuss **discuter**
to forget **oublier**
to rain **pleuvoir**

according to **selon**
convenient **pratique**
in cash **en espèces, en liquide**
safe **sûr(e)**

bank **la banque**
teller **le (la) caissier (caissière)**
banker *(officer of a bank)* **le banquier**
    (no f.: **elle est banquier)**
guard **le garde** *(no f.:* **elle est
    garde)**
employee **l'employé(e)**
customer **le (la) client(e)**
window *(of a teller)* **le guichet**
ledge **le bord**
waste basket **la corbeille à papier**
clock **la pendule**
money **l'argent** *(m.)*
cash **l'argent liquide**
change **la monnaie**
loan **l'emprunt** *(m.)*
bill *(bank note)* **le billet de banque**
bill *(money due)* **la facture**
check **le chèque**
passbook **le livret de caisse
    d'épargne**
check book **le carnet de chèques**

savings account **le compte
    d'épargne**
checking account **le compte de
    chèque**
traveler's check **le chèque de voyage**
stock *(market share)* **l'action** *(f.)*
stock market **la bourse**
deposit slip **le bordereau de
    versement**
withdrawal slip **le bordereau de
    retrait**
interest *(money paid or charged)*
    l'intérêt *(m.)*
mortgage **l'hypothèque** *(f.)*
interest rate **le taux d'intérêt**
safe, vault **le coffre fort**
safe-deposit box **le coffre (à la
    banque)**
blank, form **le formulaire**
extra charge **le supplément**
service **le service**
purse, handbag **le sac à main**
wallet **le portefeuille**

banking hours **les heures
    d'ouverture et de fermeture des
    banques**
time *(occasion)* **la fois**
sign **l'affiche** *(f.)*
pro and con **le pour et le contre**
weather **le temps**
umbrella **la parapluie**

À la banque

32

Analyse de l'illustration

1. Combien de personnes y a-t-il dans la banque?
2. Quel temps fait-il aujourd'hui?
3. De quoi discutent les gens assis à droite selon vous?
4. Où est la corbeille à papier?
5. Est-ce que les employés s'apprêtent à rentrer chez eux? Pourquoi? Comment le savez-vous?
6. Où les clients font-ils la queue?
7. Que fait le monsieur au premier plan?
8. Une cliente a oublié quelquechose. Qu'a-t-elle oublié? Et où?
9. À quoi l'affiche fait-elle référence?
10. Que semble faire l'homme près de la table?
11. Où est le garde?

Points de départ

12. Combien d'argent avez-vous dans votre portefeuille aujourd'hui, et que pensez-vous en faire?
13. Comment dépose-t-on de l'argent à la banque, et comment le retire-t-on de la banque?
14. Quels sont les avantages d'un compte en banque?
15. D'habitude, quelles sont les heures d'ouverture et de fermeture des banques?
16. En général, pourquoi allez-vous à la banque?
17. Qu'est-ce qu'un intérêt? Quand est-il payé et quand est-il perçu?
18. Quels sont les avantages des chèques de voyage?
19. Comment touche-t-on un chèque?
20. Si vous aviez beaucoup d'argent à placer, comment le placeriez-vous?

Sujets de discussion

1. Comment fonctionne une banque.
2. Travailler dans une banque: avantages et inconvénients.
3. Le pour et le contre d'avoir un coffre à la banque.

Imaginons et discutons!

A group of students accompanied by their teacher go on an authorized tour of a local bank. As they walk through the bank, employees answer their questions and explain briefly the various services of the bank.

Enact this situation in French.

to go **aller**
to walk **marcher** *(intr.)*, **promener**
    (tr.)
to continue **continuer**
to cross **traverser**
to turn **tourner**
to stop *(tr.)* **arrêter**
to stop *(intr.)* **s'arrêter**
to push **pousser**
to obey **obéir (à)**
to protect **protéger**
to jog **faire du jogging**
to wear; to carry **porter**
to live **vivre; habiter**
to tell, relate **raconter**
to be seated **être assis(e)**
to sit down **s'asseoir**
to feed **nourrir, donner à manger**
    (à)
to try (to) **essayer (de)**

red **rouge**
yellow **jaune**
green **vert(e)**
polluted **pollué(e)**
noisy **bruyant(e)**

main square, town square **la grande
    place**
small square **la petite place**
little park **le square**
downtown **le centre ville, en ville**
city **la ville**
district **le quartier**
town **la petite ville**
village **le village**
street **la rue**
street intersection **le carrefour;
    le croisement**
block *(of buildings or houses)* **le pâté
    de maisons**
traffic light **le(s) feu(x) (de
    signalisation)**
sidewalk **le trottoir**
pedestrian **le (la) piéton (piétonne)**
vehicle **le véhicule**
car **la voiture**
bike **le vélo**
motorcycle **la motocyclette, la moto**

motorcyclist **le (la) motocycliste**
motor **le moteur**
policeman **l'agent** *(m.)* **(de police)**
    (no f.: **elle est agent de police)**
traffic accident **l'accident** *(m.)* **(de la
    route), l'accident (de la
    circulation)**
helmet **le casque**
runner **le (la) coureur (coureuse)**
baby carriage **le landau**
newspaper **le journal**
store **le magasin**
theater **le théâtre**
church **l'église** *(f.)*
entertainment **la distraction** *(often
    pl.)*
awning **l'auvent** *(m.)*
bench **le banc**
fountain **la fontaine**
water **l'eau** *(f.)*
tree **l'arbre** *(m.)*
flower **la fleur**

grass **l'herbe** *(f.)*
gutter **le caniveau**
pigeon **le pigeon**

En ville

33

Analyse de l'illustration

1. Que fait le jeune homme à gauche?
2. Que regarde l'agent de police?
3. Que fait la dame que nous voyons derrière l'agent de police sur le trottoir?
4. Quelles sortes de véhicules voit-on dans la rue?
5. Que fait le petit garçon sur le trottoir?
6. Pourquoi le motocycliste porte-t-il un casque?
7. Que peut-il y avoir dans la fontaine?
8. Que fait le monsieur assis sur le banc?
9. Pourquoi l'homme assis sur le banc est-il venu en ville?
10. Décrivez la petite place.
11. Que voit-on à l'arrière plan?
12. De quelles couleurs seraient les choses que nous voyons si l'illustration était en couleur?

Points de départ

13. Qu'est-ce qu'un piéton?
14. Quelles sont les trois couleurs des feux de signalisation et que signifient-elles?
15. Pourquoi doit-on obéir aux feux de signalisation?
16. Quelles différences y a-t-il entre une bicyclette et une motocyclette?
17. À quoi servent les caniveaux?
18. Décrivez le centre de la ville (ou du village) où vous vivez.
19. Préférez-vous vivre dans une ville ou dans un village? Pourquoi?
20. À votre avis, qu'est-ce qui est le plus dangereux: faire du vélo ou conduire une voiture?

Sujets de discussion

1. Faire du jogging en ville.
2. Mon quartier préféré.
3. Habiter en centre ville: avantages et inconvénients.

Imaginons et discutons!

The tranquil scene on the preceding page changes a few seconds later when the motorcycle collides with a vehicle whose driver had stopped to ask directions. It is only a minor accident, but while the policeman handles the situation all the others in the illustration gather to discuss what they saw (or did not see). Each has a different view of what happened.

Enact the entire incident in French.

to catch fire **prendre feu**
to burn (down) **brûler (complètement)**
to set on fire **mettre le feu (à)**
to put out (a fire) **éteindre**
to asphyxiate **asphyxier, étouffer**
to rescue **sauver**
to destroy **détruire**
to run a risk **courir un risque**
to fall (down) **tomber**
to notify, summon **appeler, avertir**
to tell, let know **prévenir**
to connect **attacher**
to protect **(se) protéger**
to shout **crier**
to escape **s'échapper**
to take, transport **porter, transporter**
to collapse **s'effondrer**
to photograph **photographier**

fireproof **ininflammable**
daily **quotidien (quotidienne)**
terrible **affreux (affreuse)**
dangerous **dangereux (dangereuse)**
courageous **courageux (courageuse)**

flame **la flamme**
fire **le feu, l'incendie** (m.)
fire! **au feu!**
firefighter **le pompier, le sapeur pompier** (no f.: **elle est pompier**)
fire department **les pompiers**
firehouse **la caserne de pompiers**
fire engine **la voiture de pompiers**
arsonist, firebug **le (la) pyromane**
fire alarm box **l'avertisseur** (m.) **d'incendie** (m.)
fire drill **l'exercice** (m.) **de sauvetage**
fire extinguisher **l'extincteur** (m.)
fire hydrant **la bouche d'incendie** (m.)
dormitory (of a school) **la résidence universitaire**
alarm **l'alarme** (f.) , **l'alerte** (f.)
emergency exit **la sortie de secours**
emergency stairway **l'escalier** (m.) **de secours**

smoke **la fumée**
hose **le tuyau**
ladder **l'échelle** (f.)
siren **la sirène**
ambulance **l'ambulance** (f.)
hospital **l'hôpital** (m.)
victim **la victime**
danger **le danger**
helmet **le casque**
coat **le manteau**
equipment **l'équipement** (m.)
building **le bâtiment**
wall **le mur**
roof **le toit**
water **l'eau** (f.)
telephone **le téléphone**
arm **le bras**
photographer **le (la) photographe**

Au feu!

34

Analyse de l'illustration

1. Qu'est-ce qui semble être arrivé à la victime qui est dans les bras du pompier?
2. Que va faire le pompier au premier plan? Que semble-t-il crier?
3. Décrivez ce qui se passe dans la voiture de pompiers.
4. On voit deux échelles. Où sont-elles?
5. Que fait le photographe?
6. L'incendie va-t-il détruire le bâtiment? Comment le savez-vous?
7. Que feriez-vous si vous étiez sur le toit du bâtiment en train de brûler?

Points de départ

8. Comment peut-on éteindre un petit feu?
9. Que faut-il faire en cas d'incendie?
10. Quels risques les pompiers courent-ils?
11. Comment les pompiers se protègent-ils?
12. Qu'est-ce qu'une caserne de pompiers?
13. À quoi le pompier attache-t-il le tuyau de la voiture de pompiers pour avoir de l'eau?
14. Pour quelle raison les pompiers se servent-ils d'une échelle?
15. À quoi sert une ambulance?
16. Quel est l'équipement d'une voiture de pompiers?
17. Qu'est-ce qu'un(e) pyromane?
18. À quoi servent les exercices de sauvetage?
19. En cas d'incendie, comment vous échapperiez-vous du bâtiment où vous êtes en ce moment?
20. Expliquez la phrase «Il n'y a pas de fumée sans feu.»

Sujets de discussion

1. Un incendie que j'ai vu.
2. La prévention des incendies.
3. La vie quotidienne d'un pompier.

Imaginons et discutons!

The fire alarm has gone off in your school's largest dormitory and it is not a drill. Smoke is everywhere and shouts are heard from inside the building. As the fire engines arrive and the firefighters go to work, students who escaped the fire gather outside and exchange stories and concern for those still inside.

Enact this situation in French.

to get sick **tomber malade**
to get a sickness **contracter une maladie**
to treat *(an illness)* **soigner**
to take someone's pulse **prendre le pouls de quelqu'un**
to take someone's temperature **prendre la température de quelqu'un**
to read the temperature **lire le thermomètre**
to stay, remain **rester**
to live **habiter, vivre**
to visit **rendre visite à**
to die **mourir**
to suppose **supposer**
to listen (to) **écouter**
to examine *(patient)* **examiner, ausculter**
to meet **rencontrer**
to be *(health)* **se porter**
to be better *(of health)* **aller mieux**
to be better (+ *inf.*) **valoir mieux (+ inf.)**
to be better (than) **valoir mieux (que)**
to inoculate (against) **vacciner (contre)**

injured **blessé(e)**
sick **malade**
healthy **en bonne santé, sain(e)**
dead **mort(e)**
nowadays **de nos jours**
serious *(illness)* **sérieux (sérieuse), grave**
seriously **gravement**
rather **plutôt**
thanks to **grâce à**
close by **à côté**
private **privé(e)**

hospital **l'hôpital** *(m.)*
sanitarium **la maison de repos, le sanatorium**
infirmary **l'infirmerie** *(f.)*
doctor *(physician)* **le docteur, le médecin** *(no fem.: elle est docteur)*
nurse **l'infirmier (infirmière)**
paramedic **l'auxiliaire médical(e)**
first aid **les premiers secours**
head **la tête**
chair **la chaise**
function **la fonction**
patient **le (la) malade**
smock *(white gown of doctor)* **la blouse de médecin**
medicine **la médecine, le médicament**
thermometer **le thermomètre**
stethoscope **le stéthoscope**
bandage **le bandage, le pansement**
room **la chambre**

private room **la chambre particulière, la chambre privée**
semiprivate room **la chambre semi-privée**
ward **la salle commune**
bed **le lit**
sheet *(of linen)* **le drap**
sheet *(mattress cover)* **l'alaise** *(f.)*
medical report **la feuille d'observations**
night table **la table de nuit**
tray **le plateau**
visitor **le (la) visiteur (visiteuse)**
visiting hours **les heures de visite**
flower **la fleur**
injury **la blessure**
sickness, disease **la maladie**
accident **l'accident** *(m.)*
vaccination **la vaccination**
smallpox **la variole**
appendicitis **l'appendicite** *(f.)*
medical insurance **l'assurance** *(f.)* **médicale**

heart **le cœur**
heart attack **la crise cardiaque**
wrist **le poignet**
arm **le bras**
watch **la montre**
wrist watch **le bracelet-montre**
condition **l'état**
convalescence **la convalescence**

À l'hôpital

35

1. Pourquoi l'infirmière a-t-elle un bracelet-montre?
2. Que fait l'infirmière?
3. Que fait le docteur?
4. Décrivez le docteur sur le dessin.
5. Qu'est-ce qui vous fait penser que le malade est blessé et non pas malade?
6. Pourquoi ne pouvons-nous pas voir le bras droit du malade?
7. Dans quel état est-il?
8. Quels sont les autres objets que vous voyez dans la pièce?

Points de départ

9. Comment vous portez-vous aujourd'hui?
10. Jusqu'à quel âge espérez-vous vivre?
11. Si vous étiez sérieusement malade, pourquoi vaudrait-il mieux que vous soyez soigné(e) à l'hôpital que chez vous?
12. Qu'est-ce qu'une assurance médicale?
13. Quelle est la différence entre un hôpital et une maison de repos?
14. Qu'est-ce qu'une salle commune? Une chambre privée? Une chambre semi-privée?
15. Quelles sont les heures de visite d'un hôpital?
16. Quelles sont les fonctions d'un(e) auxiliaire médical(e)?
17. Comment prend-on le pouls?
18. Dans un hôpital on voit souvent les docteurs avec des stéthoscopes. Que fait-on avec un stéthoscope?
19. Pourquoi est-ce qu'une crise cardiaque est quelque chose de très grave?
20. Quelle maladie grave n'existe plus de nos jours grâce aux vaccinations?

Sujets de discussion

1. Les progrès de la médecine moderne.
2. Un accident sérieux que j'ai eu ou dont j'ai eu connaissance.
3. Un(e) infirmier (infirmière) m'a raconté…

Imaginons et discutons!

In a semiprivate room of a hospital, two patients and their visitors are conversing with a nurse and a doctor. We learn why each patient is there, why the doctor and nurse are in attendance, and who the visitors are.

Enact this scene in French.

to examine **examiner**
to get examined **se faire examiner**
to treat, attend to *(medical)* **soigner**
to brush (one's teeth) **se laver,**
    se brosser (les dents)
to clean *(teeth)* **nettoyer**
to find **trouver**
to count **compter**
to remove **enlever**
to fill *(a cavity)* **plomber**
to contain **contenir**
to extract **extraire**
to straighten *(teeth)* **rectifier**
to give an injection **faire une piqûre**
to break **casser**
to inflict pain (to) **faire mal (à)**
to hurt *(intr.)* **avoir mal**
to take **prendre**
to take care of **prendre soin de**
to be afraid (of) **avoir peur (de)**
to decline **refuser**

next to **à côté de**
painful **douloureux (douloureuse)**
worse **pire**
without **sans**
worried **inquiet (inquiète)**

dentist **le (la) dentiste**
dentistry *(field of study)* **les études dentaires**
dentist's office **le cabinet dentaire**
office hours **les heures de travail**
waiting room **la salle d'attente**
dental technician **l'aide-dentiste** *(m. and f.)*
dentist's chair **le fauteuil de dentiste**
patient **le (la) patient(e)**
mouth **la bouche**
gum **la gencive**
tooth **la dent**
(set of) teeth **la denture**
denture, false teeth **le dentier**
wisdom tooth **la dent de sagesse**
toothache **le mal de dents**
drill **la roulette**
filling **le plombage**
cavity **la carie, la cavité**
crown **la couronne**
brace **l'appareil dentaire** *(m.)*
sickness **la maladie**

local anesthetic **la piqûre anesthésique**
X-ray **la radiographie**
diagnosis **le diagnostic**
wax **la cire**
impression **l'empreinte** *(f.),* **le moulage**
toothbrush **la brosse à dents**
toothpaste **le dentifrice**
paper cup **le gobelet de papier**
water **l'eau** *(f.)*
arm **le bras**
armrest **l'accoudoir** *(m.)*
visit, call **la visite**

Chez le dentiste

36

1. Qui sont les deux personnes sur le dessin?
2. Quelles sont, à votre avis, les heures de travail de ce cabinet dentaire?
3. Décrivez l'expression sur la figure du jeune patient.
4. Que contient le gobelet de papier à côté de lui? À quoi sert-il?
5. Où sont les bras du jeune garçon?
6. Que va faire la dentiste?

Points de départ

7. Combien de dents a-t-on normalement sans compter les dents de sagesse?
8. Quand est-il nécessaire de porter un dentier?
9. À quoi servent les appareils dentaires?
10. À quoi servent les moulages en cire?
11. Un(e) dentiste soigne les caries. Que fait-il (elle) d'autre?
12. Quand emploie-t-on une brosse à dents et du dentifrice? Dans quel but?
13. Quand est-ce que le (la) dentiste extrait une dent?
14. Quand est-ce que le (la) dentiste doit faire une piqûre anesthésique?
15. À quoi servent les radiographies en général?
16. Quand un(e) dentiste pose-t-il (elle) une couronne?
17. Pourquoi est-il important de prendre soin de ses dents?
18. Combien de fois par an devrait-on aller chez son (sa) dentiste?
19. Pourquoi aimez-vous (ou n'aimez-vous pas) aller chez votre dentiste?
20. Pourquoi aimeriez-vous (ou n'aimeriez-vous pas) être dentiste?

Sujets de discussion

1. Comment prendre soin de ses dents.
2. Une visite chez votre dentiste.
3. Dans la salle d'attente d'un cabinet dentaire.

★ ★

**Imaginons et
discutons!**

★

Four members of a family of various ages went to the dentist. To console and advise one another, they discuss their experiences.

Enact this discussion in French.

to persuade **persuader, convaincre**
to vote **voter**
to strike **faire la grève**
to go on strike **se mettre en grève**
to give a speech **faire un discours**
to debate **débattre, discuter**
to plead **plaider**
to preach **prêcher**
to listen **écouter**
to speak (to) **s'adresser à**
to agree (with) **être du même avis,
    être d'accord (avec)**
to disagree (with) **être en désaccord
    (avec), ne pas être d'accord
    (avec)**
to sway **influencer, gouverner**
to assure **assurer**
to carry **porter**
to work **travailler**
to feel **sentir**
to depict **représenter, décrire**
to try **essayer**
to be alike **se ressembler**

on strike **en grève**
in private **en privé**
democratic **démocratique,
    démocrate**
republican **républicain(e)**
relative **relatif (relative)**
extemporaneous **improvisé(e)**
to the right **à droite, de droite**
in favor of **en faveur de**
innocent **innocent(e)**

policeman **l'agent (de police)** *(m.
    and f.)*
election **l'élection** *(f.)*
voter **l'électeur (électrice)**
voting booth **l'isoloir** *(m.)*
curtain **le rideau**
privacy **l'isolement** *(m.)*
worker **l'ouvrier (ouvrière)**
factory **l'usine** *(f.)*
union *(of workers)* **le syndicat**
sign **l'affiche** *(f.)*, **la pancarte**
subject *(of argument)* **l'objet** *(m.)*
student **l'étudiant(e)**
student leader **le (la) délégué(e)**
speech **le discours**
freedom of speech **la liberté de
    parole**
debate **le débat**
speaker **l'orateur (oratrice)**
microphone **le micro**
politician **le (la) politicien
    (politicienne), l'homme** *(m.)*
    politique

(political) party **le parti (politique)**
right *(privilege)* **le droit, le privilège**
ballot box **l'urne** *(f.)*
secret ballot **le scrutin secret**
(written) ballot **le bulletin de vote**
judge **le juge** *(no f.:* **elle est juge)**
district attorney **le procureur de la
    république**
lawyer, attorney **l'avocat(e)**
courtroom **la cour**
jury **le jury**
robe **la robe**
clergyman **l'écclésiastique** *(m.)*
sermon **le sermon**
pulpit **la chaire**
congregation **les fidèles**
assembly **l'assemblée** *(f.)*
audience **le public**
meeting **la réunion**
building **le bâtiment**
side **le côté**
fence **la clôture**

action **la scène**
drawback **l'inconvénient** *(m.)*

L'art de persuader

37

Analyse de l'illustration

1. Pourquoi est-ce que l'isoloir a des rideaux?
2. Qu'est-ce qu'il y a de l'autre côté de la clôture?
3. Pourquoi l'ouvrier porte-t-il une pancarte?
4. Qu'est-ce qui nous fait penser que le dessin de droite représente une réunion d'étudiants sur le campus d'une université?
5. Que fait le délégué des étudiants?
6. Les étudiants semblent-ils être d'accord avec leur délégué?
7. Quelle est la différence entre le discours de la politicienne et celui du délégué des étudiants?
8. Avec qui l'avocat plaide-t-il? Où la scène a-t-elle lieu?
9. Quelles personnes portent des robes?
10. Pourquoi y a-t-il un agent de police sur le dessin qui représente un isoloir?
11. D'où l'écclésiastique prêche-t-il et à qui s'addresse-t-il?

Points de départ

12. Quels sont les deux partis politiques pour lesquels le peuple américain doit généralement voter pendant les élections?
13. Qu'est-ce qu'un syndicat?
14. Que veut dire l'expression «faire la grève»?
15. Expliquez en détail ce que vous faites quand vous allez voter.
16. Quelle est la différence entre ces trois mots: assemblée, audience, congrégation?
17. Quelle est la différence entre «prêcher» et «discuter», ou entre un «sermon» et un «discours»?
18. Quels sont les points communs entre un ecclésiastique, un(e) politicien (politicienne) et un(e) avocat (avocate)?
19. Choisissez un des orateurs (ou l'oratrice) de l'illustration et dites-nous de quoi il (elle) veut persuader son audience.
20. Essayez de persuader les ouvriers de ne pas faire la grève.

Sujets de discussion

1. La liberté de parole.
2. L'art de persuader.
3. Un débat.

Imaginons et discutons!

Three student leaders are candidates in campus elections and agree to have a debate in your French class. After all three candidates state their platforms in short speeches, they challenge one another with questions and commentaries and take questions from the class.

Enact this situation in French.

to advertise **faire de la réclame,
faire de la publicité**
to offer **offrir**
to be worthwhile, pay **rapporter,
valoir la peine**
to place **mettre, placer**
to try (to) **essayer (de)**
to succeed **réussir**
to use **employer, utiliser**
to look for **chercher**
to leave **quitter**
to agree **être d'accord**
to help **aider**
to increase **augmenter**

effective **efficace**
convincing **convaincant(e)**
friendly **aimable**
smart **intelligent(e)**
frequently **fréquemment**
commonly **couramment**

salesmanship **l'art** *(m.)* **de la vente**
salesperson **le (la) vendeur
(vendeuse)**
sale **la vente**
sales, selling **les ventes**
commission **la commission**
employment, job **l'emploi** *(m.)*
company **la compagnie, la société**
free enterprise **la libre entreprise**
product **le produit**
advertising **la publicité, la réclame**
means of advertising **le média
publicitaire**
propaganda **la propagande**
advertisement **la publicité**
classified ad **la petite annonce**
billboard, sign **le panneau
publicitaire**
slogan **le slogan**
radio announcer **le (la) présentateur
(présentatrice) (à la radio)**

television announcer
**le (la) présentateur
(présentatrice) (à la télévision);
le (la) speaker (speakerine)**
script **le script, le texte**
television set **le téléviseur**
screen **l'écran** *(m.)*
(television) commercial **la publicité,
la "pub"**
quality **la qualité**
clock **l'horloge** *(f.)*
(clock) time **l'heure** *(f.)*
real estate broker **l'agent** *(m.)*
immobilier
married couple **le ménage**

L'art de la vente

38

Analyse de l'illustration

1. Sur quelle illustration peut-on voir une horloge?
2. Que lit la speakerine à votre avis?
3. Aidez-vous de ce que vous voyez sur l'écran de téléviseur pour inventer une publicité.
4. Est-il efficace de mettre des panneaux publicitaires sur les autoroutes? Pourquoi?
5. Le panneau est-il bien placé? Expliquez votre réponse.
6. Que dit la publicité sur ce panneau? Inventez.
7. Qu'est-ce qui nous fait penser que ce couple vient d'acheter une maison?

Points de départ

8. Pour quelles sortes de produits fait-on fréquemment de la publicité à la télévision?
9. Comment sait-on si une réclame a été efficace?
10. Le slogan est un média publicitaire. Donnez en français deux slogans couramment employés aux Etats-Unis.
11. «La publicité, ça rapporte.» Expliquez cette phrase.
12. Vous voulez vendre quelque chose. Inventez une petite annonce pour un magazine local.
13. Vous cherchez un emploi: inventez une petite annonce pour un journal.
14. Expliquez ce qu'est une commission.
15. Expliquez la différence entre la publicité et la propagande.
16. Qu'est-ce que la libre entreprise?
17. Aimeriez-vous être vendeur (vendeuse) dans une grande société? Pourquoi?
18. Citez quelques qualités personnelles importantes pour vendre.
19. Essayez de vendre quelque chose à votre professeur de français.
20. Consultez votre montre et dites-nous l'heure qu'il est.

Sujets de discussion

1. L'art de la vente.
2. Inventez une réclame d'une page entière.
3. Inventez un texte d'une minute pour une publicité télévisée.

★ ★

Imaginons et discutons!

★

Salesmanship is an art, and the key to success is persuasion, for everybody sells something; if not a product, then himself or herself. Keeping this in mind, work with a group to create a situation in which—as subtly as possible—all participants are attempting to evoke a favorable response from some or all of the others.

Enact the scene in French.

to type **taper à la machine**
to dictate **dicter**
to take dictation **prendre en dictée**
to photocopy **photocopier**
to press **appuyer (sur)**
to influence **influencer**
to identify **identifier**
to persuade **persuader, convaincre**
to sell **vendre**
to promote *(sales)* **promouvoir**
to get out **sortir**
to get along well (with) **s'entendre
    (avec)**
to file **classer**
to store **conserver, stocker**
to export **exporter**
to import **importer**
to coordinate **coordonner**

bilingual **bilingue**
useful **utile**
trilingual **trilingue**

business office **le bureau**
businessman **l'homme d'affaires**
businesswoman **la femme d'affaires**
business executive **le cadre** *(no fem.:*
    elle est cadre)
boss **le (la) patron (patronne)**
salesperson *(in a store)*
    le (la) vendeur (vendeuse)
company representative
    le (la) représentant(e)
sales manager **le (la) directeur
    (directrice) commerciale**
appointment **le rendez-vous**
sale, sales, selling **la vente, les ventes**
salesmanship **l'art** *(m.)* **de la vente**
company, firm **la société**
management **la gestion, la direction**
employee **l'employé(e)**
office work **le travail de bureau**
office worker **l'employé(e) de bureau**
secretary **le (la) secrétaire**
computer operator **l'opérateur
    (opératrice) de saisie**
computer **l'ordinateur** *(m.)*
data **la donnée**

screen **l'écran** *(m.)*
computer science, data processing
    l'informatique *(f.)*
office machine **la machine de bureau**
typewriter **la machine à écrire**
typist **le (la) dactylo**
typing **la dactylographie**
steonotypist **le (la) sténodactylo**
shorthand **la sténographie**
typing and shorthand
    la sténo-dactylographie
dictation **la dictée**
dictating machine **le dictaphone**
file, folder **le dossier**
filing cabinet **le classeur**
card-index file **le fichier**
report **le rapport**
photocopier **le photocopieur**
photocopy **la photocopie**
word processor **la machine à
    traitement de texte**
desk **le bureau**
drawer (of a desk) **le tiroir**
wastebasket **la corbeille à papier**
button **le bouton**

key *(of key board)* **la touche**
market **le marché, le débouché**
product **le produit**
map **la carte**
map of the world **la mappemonde,
    le planisphère**
customer **le (la) client(e)**
contract **le contrat**
invoice **la facture**
working hours **les heures de travail**
(foreign) language **la langue (étrangère)**
foreign trade **le commerce
    international**
Asia **l'Asie** *(f.)*
Africa **l'Afrique** *(f.)*
Australia **l'Australie** *(f.)*
Europe **l'Europe** *(f.)*
export **l'exportation** *(f.)*
import **l'importation** *(f.)*
advertising **la publicité**
sales promotion **la promotion des
    ventes**
business administration *(field of study)*
    la gestion et l'administration
free enterprise **la libre entreprise**

Au bureau

39

Analyse de l'illustration

1. Quels continents pouvez-vous identifier sur la carte?
2. À quoi sert la machine qui se trouve sous la carte?
3. Que fait la directrice dans le bureau à l'arrière-plan?
4. Que fait la secrétaire?
5. Où se trouve la corbeille à papier?
6. Où peut-on garder les dossiers ou les rapports?
7. Expliquez ce que fait un(e) opérateur (opératrice) de saisie.
8. L'homme qui est en train de sortir est directeur commercial de cette companie. À votre avis, où va-t-il?
9. Où peuvent bien être les autres employés de bureau?
10. Pourquoi y a-t-il une mappemonde sur le mur du bureau?

Points de départ

11. Quelles sont les heures de travail des employés de bureau en général?
12. Expliquez la différence entre un(e) dactylo et un(e) secrétaire.
13. Aimeriez-vous être représentant(e)? Pourquoi?
14. Pourquoi est-il très utile d'avoir un ordinateur?
15. Qu'est-ce qu'une secrétaire trilingue?
16. Pourquoi est-il utile à un(e) étudiant(e) de gestion et d'administration de savoir parler français?
17. Qu'est-ce qu'un(e) client(e)? Qu'est-ce qu'une facture?
18. Expliquez ce qu'est un bon débouché.
19. L'art de la vente: qu'est-ce que c'est?
20. Que veut dire l'expression «la libre entreprise»?

Sujets de discussion

1. La journée d'un(e) secrétaire.
2. Le travail de bureau.
3. Un rendez-vous d'affaires.

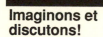

Imaginons et discutons!

The boss is off on a business trip and you and your co-workers have the office to yourselves. It's time for some speculation about office procedures and a little gossiping.

Enact this discussion in French.

to employ **employer**
to become self-employed **s'établir à son compte**
to be self-employed **travailler à son compte**
to earn **gagner**
to earn one's living **gagner sa vie**
to look for, seek **chercher**
to offer **offrir**
to register (with, at) **s'inscrire (à)**
to start *(a new job)* **commencer**
to expect **s'attendre à**
to undertake *(work)* **entreprendre** *(un travail)*
to be found **se trouver**
to graduate *(from college, university)* **obtenir ses diplômes**
to enter a career **commencer une carrière**
to look (at) **regarder**
to name **nommer**
to prepare **préparer**
to participate (in) **prendre part (à)**
to define **définir**
to draw up **préparer**
to ask (someone) questions **poser des questions (à quelqu'un)**

till now **jusqu'à présent**
ambitious **ambitieux (ambitieuse)**
hardworking **travailleur (travailleuse)**

employment agency, placement bureau **le bureau de placement**
recruiter, placement agent **l'orienteur (orienteuse)**
employment, job **l'emploi** *(m.),* **le métier**
employer **l'employeur (employeuse)**
boss **le (la) patron (patronne)**
employee **l'employé(e)**
company, firm **la société**
work **le travail**
candidate **le (la) candidat(e)**
interview **l'interview** *(f.)*
résumé, dossier **le curriculum vitae, le C.V.**
salary **le salaire**
facts, information **les renseignements**
part-time work **le travail à mi-temps**
moonlighting, extra work **le deuxième emploi**
Bachelor's degree **la licence**

major *(course of study)* **la spécialité**
career **la carrière**
classified ads **les petites annonces**
newspaper **le journal**
want ad **l'annonce** *(f.),* **l'offre** *(f.)* **d'emploi** *(m.)*
sales department **le service des ventes**
sales clerk **le (la) vendeur (vendeuse)**
sales representative **le (la) représentant(e)**
foreign department **le service international**
goal, plan **le plan, le but**
success **le succès**
waiting room **la salle d'attente**
desk **le bureau**
notebook **le carnet**
memo pad **le bloc (de papier)**
ring binder **le classeur**
filing card **la fiche**
filing case, filing box **le fichier**

(ball-point) pen **le stylo (à bille)**
future **l'avenir** *(m.)*

À l'agence pour l'emploi

40

Analyse de l'illustration

1. Quels objets voyez-vous sur le bureau?
2. Le monsieur qui nous regarde est-il un candidat ou un employé? Comment le savez-vous?
3. Que font les candidat(e)s dans la salle d'attente?
4. De quoi discutent la dame et le monsieur au premier plan?

Points de départ

5. Expliquez ce qu'est un bureau de placement.
6. Qu'est-ce qu'une «offre d'emploi»?
7. Quand serez-vous prêt(e) à commencer l'emploi?
8. Quelle est votre spécialité?
9. Quel genre de travail chercherez-vous lorsque vous aurez obtenu vos diplômes?
10. À quel salaire vous attendez-vous au début?
11. Quelles sont vos aptitudes pour le service international?
12. Pourquoi (ne) voulez-vous (pas) travailler à l'étranger?
13. Quel travail à mi-temps avez-vous eu jusqu'à présent?
14. Pourquoi tant de gens doivent-ils prendre un deuxième emploi?
15. Qu'est-ce qu'une interview?
16. Pourquoi (ne) vous êtes-vous (pas) inscrit(e) au bureau de placement de votre école ou de votre université?
17. Quels renseignements devraient se trouver dans un C.V.?
18. Quels sont vos plans pour l'avenir?
19. Quelle est votre définition du mot «succès»?
20. Pourquoi voulez-vous (ne voulez-vous pas) travailler à votre compte?

Sujets de discussion

1. Un métier que j'aime particulièrement.
2. Comment préparer un curriculum vitae.
3. Mes plans pour l'avenir.

Imaginons et discutons!

There you are, face to face with a recruiter. You want a job with his company, but it won't be easy because the competition is keen. You ask questions about the position. He wants to know about your qualifications and goals.

Enact this interview in French.

81

to publish **publier**
to manage **diriger**
to cover, report **faire un reportage (sur)**
to edit **éditer, rédiger**
to correct **corriger**
to type **taper à la machine**
to telephone **téléphoner (à)**
to be on the phone **être au téléphone**
to carry on *(job)* **exercer un métier**
to depict **représenter, décrire**

foreign **étranger (étrangère)**
required **requis(e)**
world *(adj.)* **mondial(e)**
only **seulement**
interesting **intéressant(e)**
amusing **amusant(e)**

editorial room, newspaper office **le bureau de rédaction**
telephone **le téléphone**
teletype **le téléscripteur**
typewriter **la machine à écrire**
eyeshade **la visière**
photograph **la photo, la photographie**
office **le bureau**
boss **le chef; le (la) patron (patronne)**
newspaper **le journal**
newspaperman **le journaliste**
newspaperwoman **la journaliste**
journalism **le journalisme**
reporter **le reporter** *(no fem.: elle est reporter)*
editor **le (la) rédacteur (rédactrice)**
city editor **l'editorialiste des nouvelles locales** *(m. and f.)*
editor-in-chief **le (la) rédacteur (rédactrice) en chef**

foreign language **la langue étrangère**
reader **le (la) lecteur (lectrice)**
columnist **le (la) collaborateur (collaboratrice) régulier d'un journal**
interview **l'entrevue** *(f.),* **l'interview** *(f.)*
foreign correspondent **le (la) correspondant(e) étranger (étrangère)**
qualification **la qualification**
sports **les sports** *(m. pl.)*
sports writer **le chroniqueur sportif** *(no fem.: elle est chroniqueur)*
correspondent **le (la) correspondant(e)**
proofreader **le (la) correcteur (correctrice)**
headline **le gros titre, la manchette**
press **la presse**
copy boy **le garçon de bureau**

story **l'histoire** *(f.)*
news **les nouvelles** *(f. pl.),* **les informations** *(f. pl.),* **les actualités** *(f. pl.)*
news item **la nouvelle**
dispatch **la dépêche, l'envoi** *(m.),* **l'expédition** *(f.)*
advertising **la publicité**
editorial **l'éditorial** *(m.)*
criticism, review **la critique**
front page **la première page, la une**
women's page **la page féminine**
society page **la rubrique mondaine**
magazine **le magazine, la revue**
comics **les bandes dessinées**
job, profession **le métier**
part **la section**
opinion **l'opinion** *(f.)*
envelope **l'enveloppe** *(f.)*
event **l'événement** *(m.)*
mistake **l'erreur** *(f.)*
whole **l'ensemble** *(m.)*

Dans le bureau de rédaction

41

1. Que font les deux journalistes à l'arrière-plan?
2. Que regardent les deux journalistes à gauche?
3. Que fait l'homme qui porte une visière?
4. Décrivez l'homme qui est au téléphone.
5. Où est le garçon de bureau? Que fait-il?
6. Comment savons-nous que l'illustration représente un bureau de rédaction?
7. Qui est le chef des journalistes dans cette rédaction?

Points de départ

8. Qui écrit les nouvelles locales?
9. Qui fait la chronique sportive?
10. Quelle est la différence entre un reporter et un(e) rédacteur (rédactrice)?
11. Qu'est-ce qu'un(e) correcteur (correctrice)?
12. Qu'est-ce que la manchette d'un journal?
13. Expliquez ce qu'est un éditorial.
14. Un(e) journaliste ne pourrait pas exercer son métier sans sa machine à écrire et son téléphone. Expliquez cette phrase.
15. Lisez-vous le journal tous les jours? Si non, pourquoi pas? Si oui, quel journal lisez-vous, et qu'en pensez-vous? Expliquez votre opinion.
16. En quoi un journal et un magazine sont-ils différents?
17. Quelles sont les sections d'un journal américain?
18. Quelles parties du journal lisez-vous et quelles parties ne lisez-vous pas? Expliquez.
19. Quels sont les lecteurs et les lectrices de ce livre?
20. Qui fait le reportage d'événements étrangers? Quelles sont les qualifications requises pour ce type de reportage?

Sujets de discussion

1. Un fait divers pour un journal.
2. Une entrevue avec…
3. Ce que je préfère lire dans le journal.

★ ★

Imaginons et discutons!

★

In the illustration on the preceding page, the news emerging from the teletype machine is momentous. In French, enact the scene that follows, as everyone in the illustration reacts to the event.

to perform, act, give a play **jouer**
to play a role **jouer un rôle**
to applaud **applaudir**
to raise; go up **lever; se lever**
to come down **tomber**
to leave *(intr.)* **partir, s'en aller**
to leave *(tr.)* **quitter**
to find **trouver**
to find out about, learn of
   apprendre, savoir
to tip **donner un pourboire**
to be located **être situé(e), se
   trouver**
to take, get **prendre**
to sing **chanter**
to hear **entendre**

inexpensive **bon marché; pas cher
   (chère)**
least expensive **le moins cher
   (chère)**
bearded **barbu**
to the left **à gauche**
at the beginning **au début**
at the end **à la fin**

theater **le théâtre**
play **la pièce**
playwright **le (la) dramaturge,
   l'auteur dramatique** (*no fem.:*
   elle est auteur)
title **le titre**
actor **l'acteur**
actress **l'actrice**
stage **la scène**
stage manager **le régisseur** (*no
   fem.:* **elle est régisseur**)
stagehand **le (la) machiniste**
opera **l'opéra** *(f.)*
music **la musique**
audience **les spectateurs, le public**
claque, hired clappers **la claque**
applause **les applaudissements** *(m.)*
seat **la place**
box **la loge**
box seat **le fauteuil de loge**
orchestra seat **le fauteuil d'orchestre**
balcony seat **le fauteuil de balcon**
gallery **le dernier balcon**

aisle **l'allée** *(f.)*
row **le rang, la rangée**
usher **l'ouvreur (ouvreuse)**
ticket **le ticket, le billet**
box office (ticket window)
   le guichet, le bureau de location
lobby **l'entrée** *(f.)*
intermission **l'entracte** *(m.)*
performance, show
   la représentation, le spectacle
first performance, opening night
   la première
scenery **le(s) décor(s)**
curtain *(of a stage)* **le rideau**
dressing room **la loge (d'acteur)**
act **l'acte** *(m.)*
type **le genre**
scene **la scène**
quarrel **la dispute**
(emergency) exit **la sortie de
   secours**
success **le succès**
failure, flop **le fiasco, le four**

gentleman **l'homme** *(m.)*
beard **la barbe**
head **la tête**
glasses **les lunettes** *(f. pl.)*
hat **le chapeau**
house, home **la maison, le foyer**
couch **le canapé**
chair **la chaise**
armchair **le fauteuil**
chest of drawers **la commode**
coffee table **la table basse**
chandelier **le lustre**
room *(of a house)* **la chambre,
   la pièce**
comment **la réflexion,
   le commentaire**

Au théâtre

42

Analyse de l'illustration

1. Qui ne peut pas bien voir la scène?
2. Où est la loge que l'on peut voir sur l'image?
3. Décrivez le monsieur qui s'en va.
4. Où la sortie de secours peut-elle se trouver à votre avis?
5. Quel genre de scène est-on en train de jouer à votre avis?
6. Décrivez le décor sur la scène.
7. Inventez un titre pour la pièce représentée.

Points de départ

8. Où peut-on acheter des billets de théâtre?
9. Quelles sortes de places peut-on prendre et où sont-elles situées?
10. Quelles sont les places les moins chères généralement?
11. En quoi l'ouvreur (ouvreuse) peut-il (elle) vous aider?
12. En France, on donne généralement un petit pourboire à l'ouvreur (ouvreuse). Qu'en pensez-vous?
13. Quand le rideau se lève-t-il et quand tombe-t-il?
14. Que font les machinistes?
15. Où peut-on aller pendant l'entracte?
16. Qu'est-ce qu'une «première»?
17. Comment un auteur sait-il si la première de sa pièce a été un succès ou un four?
18. Donnez le titre d'une pièce célèbre.
19. Expliquez la différence entre une pièce et un opéra.
20. En quoi une pièce est-elle différente d'un roman?

Sujets de discussion

1. Pourquoi le monsieur barbu quitte le théâtre.
2. Réflexions entendues à la première d'une pièce à succès.
3. Description d'un théâtre.

Imaginons et discutons!

You and a group of friends are at the theater together. In the lobby during an intermission, you exchange impressions of what you have seen so far: the actors, the actresses, the scenery, the play itself, and even the audience. Several of you also comment on the location of your seats.

Enact this discussion in French.

to play *(music)* **jouer, faire de la musique**
to play *(an instrument)* **jouer de**
to conduct **diriger**
to sing **chanter**
to accompany **accompagner**
to listen (to) **écouter**
to make use of **utiliser**
to belong to, be a part of **faire partie de**
to be missing **manquer**
to take off, remove **enlever**
to wear **porter**
to depict **représenter**
to adapt (to), adjust oneself (to) **s'adapter (à)**
to name **nommer**
to mean **signifier, vouloir dire**

slow(ly) **lent(e) (lentement), doux (douce) (doucement)**
moderately slow **lent(e) et modéré**
brisk **vif (vive)**
lively **animé(e)**
loud(ly) **fort(e)**
by heart **par cœur, de mémoire**
encore **bis** *(adv.)*

symphony orchestra **l'orchestre** *(m.)* **symphonique**
opera **l'opéra** *(m.)*
symphony **la symphonie**
chamber music **la musique de chambre**
musician **le (la) musicien (musicienne)**
soloist **le (la) soliste**
singer **le (la) chanteur (chanteuse)**
accompaniment **l'accompagnement** *(m.)*
conductor **le chef d'orchestre** (*no fem.: elle est chef d'orchestre*)
composer **le (la) compositeur (compositrice)**
composition, *(musical)* piece **la composition musicale**
baton **le bâton**
theater **le théâtre**
audience **les auditeurs (auditrices)** *(music)* ; **les spectateurs** *(theater)*

row **la rangée**
member **le membre** (*no fem.:* **elle est membre**)
(music) stand **le pupitre (à musique)**
note **la note**
musical score **la partition**
(article of) clothing **le vêtement**
melody **la mélodie**
harmony **l'harmonie** *(f.)*
rhythm **le rythme**
motif, theme **le thème**
movement *(of a symphony)* **le mouvement**
overture **l'ouverture** *(f.)*
prelude **le prélude**
fugue **la fugue**
piano **le piano**
grand piano **le piano à queue**
wind instrument **l'instrument** *(m.)* **à vent**
flute **la flûte**
oboe **le hautbois**

bassoon **le basson**
horn **le cor**
trumpet **la trompette**
trombone **le trombone**
clarinet **la clarinette**
tuba **le tuba**
string instrument **l'instrument à cordes**
string, cord **la corde**
bow **l'archet** *(m.)*
violin **le violon**
violoncello **le violoncelle**
viola **la viole**
harp **la harpe**
lyre **la lyre**
percussion instrument **l'instrument à percussion**
drum **le tambour**
kettledrum **la timbale**
drumstick **la baguette**
cymbal **la cymbale**
shoe **la chaussure**
quality **la qualité**

L'orchestre symphonique

43

Analyse de l'illustration

1. Combien de membres de l'orchestre peut-on voir sur l'image?
2. Combien d'instruments à vent pouvez-vous indentifier? Nommez-les.
3. Où sont les musiciens qui jouent des instruments à cordes? Et ceux qui jouent des instruments à percussion?
4. Quels sont les instruments de musique représentés sur ce dessin?
5. Que fait le chef d'orchestre avec les bras?
6. De quels instruments les femmes jouent-elles sur ce dessin?
7. Quels instruments manquent sur cette illustration d'un orchestre symphonique?
8. De quelle façon les membres de l'orchestre se servent-ils de leur pupitre?
9. Qui écoute la musique?

Points de départ

10. Si un chef d'orchestre n'a pas de pupitre ou s'il ne s'en sert pas, qu'est-ce que cela signifie?
11. Si vous étiez musicien (musicienne) dans un orchestre symphonique, de quel instrument aimeriez-vous jouer?
12. Avec quoi joue-t-on du violon? des timbales?
13. En général, combien de mouvements y a-t-il dans une symphonie?
14. Expliquez la différence entre un opéra et une symphonie.
15. Expliquez ce qu'est l'ouverture ou le prélude d'un opéra.
16. Plusieurs Français étaient de grands musiciens ou de grands compositeurs. Nommez-en un(e).
17. Expliquez la différence entre un orchestre symphonique et un orchestre de musique de chambre.
18. Quelles sont, à votre avis, les qualités les plus importantes d'un bon chef d'orchestre symphonique?
19. Quels sont les instruments d'un orchestre symphonique qui peuvent aussi s'adapter à la musique populaire ou au jazz?
20. Un des instruments les plus connus manque sur ce dessin. Lequel est-ce?

Sujets de discussion

1. Le genre de musique qui me plaît le plus.
2. L'instrument dont je sais jouer.
3. Problèmes entre un chef d'orchestre et ses musiciens.

★ ★
Imaginons et discutons!
★

Imagine that some great composers, musicians and conductors of the past are resurrected for a discussion and appraisal of the symphonic, operatic, or popular music of today.

Choose the roles and enact the fantasy in French, but avoid being too technical for listeners untrained in music.

to work for oneself **travailler à son compte**
to saw **scier**
to sew **coudre**
to build **bâtir**
to repair **réparer**
to paint **peindre**
to cut, carve **couper, découper**
to cook *(tr.)* **faire cuire, préparer**
to cook *(intr.)* **faire la cuisine**
to stir **remuer**
to wear **porter**
to employ **employer**
to earn **gagner**
to deduct **déduire, soustraire**
to lack **manquer de**
to take care (of) **s'occuper (de)**
to do *(a job)* **exercer**
to mend **raccommoder**
to dismiss, fire **renvoyer, congédier**
to present **présenter**
to depend (on) **dépendre (de)**
to end **terminer**

bald **chauve**
right-handed **droitier (droitière)**
    (adj. and noun)
risky **risqué(e)**
judging by **d'après**
seldom **rarement**
nowadays **de nos jours**
during, for **pendant**
per day (week) **par jour (semaine)**
more **davantage**

trade **le métier**
job **l'emploi** *(m.)*, **le travail**
work **le travail**
experience **l'expérience** *(f.)*
responsibility **la responsabilité**
worker, wage earner **l'ouvrier (ouvrière)**
craftsmanship **l'artisanat** *(m.)*
craftsman **l'artisan**
craftswoman **l'artisane**
employer, boss **le (la) patron (patronne), l'employeur (employeuse)**
employee **l'employé(e)**
working class **la classe ouvrière**
wages **la paye**
salary, stipend **le salaire, les appointements**
social security **les assurances** *(f.)* **sociales**
job security **la sécurité de l'emploi**
withholding tax **l'impôt** *(m.)* **sur le revenu**

overtime **les heures supplémentaires** *(f. pl.)*
profession **la profession**
tool **l'outil** *(m.)*, **l'instrument** *(m.)*
shoe **la chaussure**
shoemaker **le (la) cordonnier (cordonnière)**
carpenter **le menuisier** *(no fem.: elle est menuisier)*
saw **la scie**
board *(piece of lumber)* **la planche**
seamstress **la couturière** *(no masc.)*
needle **l'aiguille** *(f.)*
thread **le fil**
cloth, fabric **l'étoffe** *(f.)*, **le tissu**
sewing machine **la machine à coudre**
overalls **la salopette, la combinaison**
paint **la peinture**
house painter **le (la) peintre en bâtiment (femme peintre en bâtiment)**

paint brush **le pinceau**
ladder **l'échelle** *(f.)*
meat **la viande**
butcher **le (la) boucher (bouchère)**
knife **le couteau**
cook **le (la) cuisinier (cuisinière)**
pot **le pot, la marmite**
ladle **la louche**
apron **le tablier**

Les métiers

44

Analyse de l'illustration

1. De quel outil le menuisier se sert-il?
2. Que tient le menuisier dans la main gauche?
3. Que fait la couturière? De quel instrument se sert-elle?
4. Décrivez le boucher. Que fait-il?
5. Que fait le cuisinier?
6. De tous les gens que vous voyez sur l'illustration, lesquels portent des tabliers?
7. Qui est chauve ou presque chauve?
8. Que tiennent le cordonnier, le menuisier et la femme peintre dans la main droite?
9. Comment savez-vous que le boucher et le menuisier ne sont pas gauchers?
10. Lesquelles de ces six personnes travaillent à leur compte? Lesquelles travaillent pour un(e) patron (patronne)?
11. Lequel de ces six métiers préféreriez-vous exercer? Pourquoi?

Points de départ

12. Quelle est l'importance de l'artisanat de nos jours?
13. Qu'est-ce que c'est qu'un menuisier?
14. Qu'est-ce qu'un boucher et un menuisier ont en commun?
15. De nos jours un cordonnier fait rarement des chaussures. Que fait-il surtout?
16. Quand congédie-t-on un(e) employé(e)?
17. Expliquez la différence entre un(e) artisan(e) et un employé(e).
18. Combien d'heures travaille-t-on habituellement par jour et par semaine aux États-Unis?
19. Expliquez ce que sont «les heures supplémentaires».
20. Si toutes ces personnes étaient employées, l'une gagnerait davantage que les autres. Expliquez pourquoi.

Sujets de discussion

1. J'aime (je n'aime pas) travailler avec mes mains.
2. Travailler à son compte. Avantages et inconvénients.
3. Les responsabilités d'un employeur (employeuse).

★ ★ Imaginons et discutons! ★

Imagine that the six workers on the preceding page have a discussion about their jobs, their wages, and their employers. One of the six is self-employed.

Enact this discussion in French.

to collect **collectionner, faire une collection (de)**
to keep, preserve *(books, stamps, etc.)* **ranger**
to magnify **grossir**
to revolve (about) **tourner (autour de)**
to look at, to watch **regarder**
to see **voir, apercevoir**
to check **vérifier**
to take care of **s'occuper de**

current, in use **en circulation**
starry **étoilé(e)**
exotic **exotique**

pastime, hobby **le passe-temps**
collector **le (la) collectionneur (collectionneuse)**
numismatics, coin collecting **la numismatique**
philately, stamp collecting **la philatélie**
coin **la pièce (de monnaie)**
stamp **le timbre**
cent **le cent**
box **la boîte**
case, holder **l'étui** *(m.)*
magnifying glass **la loupe**
table, desk **la table**
astronomer **l'astronome** *(m. and f.)*
amateur astronomer, stargazer **l'astronome amateur** *(m. and f.)*
telescope **le télescope**
sky, heavens **le ciel**
earth **la terre**
moon **la lune**
sun **le soleil**

star **l'étoile** *(f.)*
planet **la planète** *(Mercure, Vénus, Mars, la Terre, Jupiter, Saturne, Uranus, Neptune, Pluton)*
solar system **le système solaire**
constellation **la constellation**
axis **l'axe** *(m.)*
cloud **le nuage**
shadow **l'ombre** *(f.)*
rocket **la fusée**
group **le groupe**
kind **la sorte, l'espèce** *(f.)*
stool **le tabouret**
record **le disque**
record player **le tourne-disque**
cover, jacket *(of a record)* **la pochette**
carpet **la moquette**
cat **le chat**
water **l'eau** *(f.)*
fish **le poisson**
tank *(of fish)* **l'aquarium** *(m.)*
thermometer **le thermomètre**

temperature **la température**
oxygen **l'oxygène** *(m.)*
bubble **la bulle**
aerator **l'aérateur** *(m.)*
country, nation **le pays**

Les passe-temps

45

Analyse de l'illustration

1. Avec quel instrument le collectionneur examine-t-il ses pièces?
2. Où les étuis sont-ils rangés?
3. Pourquoi y a-t-il des livres sur la table à côté des pièces?
4. Que fait la dame assise sur le tabouret?
5. Pourquoi pourrait-on dire que la nuit est favorable à l'observation du ciel?
6. Décrivez ce que vous voyez dans l'image où il y a un chat.
7. Combien de disques apercevez-vous?
8. Que collectionnent les deux personnes âgées?
9. À quoi sert l'aérateur dans l'aquarium?
10. Pourquoi y a-t-il un thermomètre dans l'aquarium?

Points de départ

11. Expliquez la différence entre la numismatique et la philatélie.
12. Quelles sont les valeurs des pièces de monnaie en circulation dans votre pays?
13. Quelle ressemblance y a-t-il entre une loupe et un télescope?
14. La terre est une planète. Qu'est-ce que le soleil?
15. La terre tourne autour du soleil et tourne aussi sur son axe. Expliquez le mouvement de la lune.
16. Qu'est-ce que le système solaire?
17. Qu'est-ce qu'une constellation?
18. Quelle sorte d'animal familier préférez-vous et pourquoi?
19. Avez-vous un aquarium? Pourquoi (pas)?
20. Que collectionnez-vous? Si vous ne collectionnez rien, quel est votre passe-temps?

Sujets de discussion

1. Mon passe-temps favori.
2. Les animaux familiers.
3. Une description simplifiée de l'univers.

Imaginons et discutons!

Most people have collected something or have a favorite pastime. By asking one another questions, elicit your classmates' hobbies or pastimes and how they got started.

Enact this discussion in French.

to build **construire**
to be handy **bricoler**
to hammer **marteler, frapper à**
    coups de marteau, enfoncer
to saw **scier**
to cut *(oneself)* **(se) couper**
to screw **visser**
to hang **accrocher**
to chop **hacher, couper en**
    morceaux
to drill *(a hole)* **percer**
to turn **tourner**
to hold (together) **tenir**
to level **aplanir**
to begin **commencer, se mettre à**

useful **utile**
useless **inutile**
at the same time **simultanément, en**
    même temps
first *(adv.)* **en premier**
last *(adv.)* **en dernier**
favorite **favori (favorite)**
awkward **maladroit(e)**

handyman **le bricoleur**
handywoman **la bricoleuse**
hobby **le passe-temps**
workbench **l'établi** *(m.)*
tool **l'outil** *(m.)*
lathe **le tour**
vice **l'étau** *(m.)*
hammer **le marteau**
saw **la scie**
miter box **la boîte à onglets**
set square **l'équerre** *(f.)*
hack saw **la scie à métaux**
screw **la vis**
screw driver **le tournevis**
nail **le clou**
plane **le rabot**
wrench **la clef anglaise**
pliers **les tenailles** *(pl.)*
cutting pliers **la pince coupante**
hatchet **la hachette**
shears **les cisailles** *(f. pl.) (metal)*
wire **le fil (de fer)**
chisel **le burin**

level **le niveau**
brace **le vilebrequin**
bit **la mèche**
crowbar **le levier, la barre de fer**
sand paper **le papier de verre,**
    le papier-émeri
T square **le té à dessin**
nut **l'écrou** *(m.)*
bolt **le boulon**
metal **le métal**
wood **le bois**
hardwood **le bois dur**
oak **le chêne**
softwood **le bois tendre**
pine **le pin**
shavings *(of wood)* **les copeaux**
    (m. pl.)
cabinet **le placard**
glue **la colle**
oil can **la burette**
size **la taille, la dimension**
piece **la pièce**
jar **le bocal,** *pl.* **les bocaux**

hole **le trou**
common factor **le point commun**
size **la taille**
construction **la construction**

Les bricoleurs

46

Analyse de l'illustration

1. Qu'est-ce que l'homme et la femme sont en train de faire?
2. Qu'apercevez-vous dans les bocaux?
3. Nommez les objets sur l'établi.
4. Quels sont les outils accrochés dans le placard?
5. Avec laquelle des deux scies l'homme sciera-t-il un morceau de métal? Avec quel outil pourrait-il couper du fil de fer?
6. Un outil très utile n'est pas sur le dessin. À votre avis quel est cet outil?
7. Dans la construction de la maison, quel outil le bricoleur a-t-il utilisé en premier et en dernier: le rabot, la scie ou le papier de verre?
8. Sur le dessin, quels outils les deux bricoleurs ne vont-ils sans doute pas utiliser?
9. Est-ce que les bricoleurs ont utilisé le ciseau ou le rabot? Comment le savez-vous?

Points de départ

10. Quel genre de bois est le plus facile à scier?
11. Que fait-on avec une hachette?
12. Qu'est-ce qu'un copeau? Quels outils font des copeaux?
13. Qu'est-ce que c'est qu'un(e) bricoleur (bricoleuse)?
14. Que fait-on avec un étau?
15. De quel instrument se sert-on avec des vis?
16. Avec quel instrument enfonce-t-on des clous?
17. Que fait-on avec un vilebrequin et une mèche? Pourquoi y a-t-il plusieurs tailles de mèches?
18. Nommez un bois dur et un bois tendre.
19. Quel est le point commun entre une clef anglaise, des tenailles et un étau? Entre un marteau et une hachette? Entre un ciseau et un rabot?
20. Quel outil doit être tenu à deux mains simultanément?

Sujets de discussion

1. Comment construire…
2. Quand les outils se mettent à parler.
3. Les bons et les mauvais bricoleurs.

Imaginons et discutons!

Having moved from a cramped, rented apartment, a young family has just bought its first house. It is an older home that needs some work, and is spacious enough to include an area for a workbench and cabinets. While in an apartment, the family had no tools, but now that they have a place to keep them—and soon may need them—they have decided to purchase some.

In French, enact the family's discussion about tools and which ones they will probably need.

to make the bed **faire le lit**
to clean **nettoyer**
to wash **laver**
to do dishes **faire la vaisselle**
to dry **sécher**
to scrub **frotter fort**
to iron **repasser**
to sweep **balayer**
to vacuum the carpet **passer
  l'aspirateur**
prepare *(food)* **préparer**
to cook *(intr.)* **faire la cuisine,
  cuisiner**
to cook *(tr.)* **faire cuire**
to protect **protéger**
to dissolve **dissoudre**
to run *(of machines)* **marcher**
accomplish, carry through **accomplir**
to differ (from) **différer (de)**
to finish **finir**

dirty **sale**
clean **propre**
right-handed **droitier (droitière)**
left-handed **gaucher (gauchère)**
tired **fatigué(e)**
broken **cassé(e)**
undoubtedly **sans doute**
household **ménager (ménagère)**

home **le foyer**
chore **la corvée**
household chores **les travaux
  ménagers** *(m. pl.)*, **les corvées
  ménagères**
household **le ménage**
housewife **la ménagère**
bed **le lit**
servant, maid **la bonne,
  le (la) domestique, l'employé(e)
  de maison**
cleaning woman **la femme de
  ménage, l'aide** *(f.)* **ménagère**
sheet **le drap**
mattress **le matelas**
pillow **l'oreiller** *(m.)*
pillowcase **la taie**
blanket **la couverture**
bedspread **le couvre-lit**
dishes **la vaisselle**
water **l'eau** *(f.)*
trash, garbage **les ordures** *(f. pl.)*

automatic dishwasher
  **le lave-vaisselle, la machine à
  laver la vaisselle**
draining rack *(for dishes)* **l'égouttoir**
  (m.)
plate **l'assiette** *(f.)*
pot **la marmite**
frying pan **la poêle**
pan **la casserole**
handle *(of a pan)* **le manche**
sink **l'évier** *(m.)*
garbage disposal **le broyeur à
  ordures**
grease **la graisse**
soap **le savon**
detergent **le détergent**
glove **le gant**
floor **le plancher**
rug **le tapis**
vacuum cleaner **l'aspirateur** *(m.)*
broom **le balai**
dustpan **la pelle à ordures**

dusting brush **la balayette**
bucket **le seau**
brush **la brosse**
wastebasket **la corbeille à papier**
automatic clothes drier **le séchoir,
  le sèche-linge**
wash **le linge, la lessive**
underwear **les sous-vêtements** *(m.
  pl.)*
clothesline **la corde à linge**
garbage can **la boîte à ordures,
  la poubelle**
sofa **le sofa, le divan**
stool **le tabouret**

Les travaux ménagers

47

1. Quels sont les travaux ménagers qui doivent être faits tous les jours?
2. Lequel des travaux représentés sur le dessin peut être fait le plus rapidement?
3. Pour quelles corvées ménagères devrait-on mettre des gants? Expliquez.
4. Où voyez-vous des oreillers sans taies?
5. Qu'est-ce que l'homme lave dans l'évier?
6. À quoi sert un égouttoir?
7. S'il y a un broyeur à ordures sur un de ces dessins, pourquoi ne peut-on pas le voir?
8. Quelles personnes sur le dessin se servent de savon ou de détergent?
9. Où sont la pelle et la balayette?
10. Des deux seaux, lequel sert de poubelle?
11. Qu'est-ce qu'il y a dans l'autre seau?

12. Pourquoi se sert-on de détergent?
13. Quand se sert-on d'un aspirateur et quand se sert-on d'une brosse?
14. À quoi sert un balai?
15. Décrivez la différence entre une marmite et une casserole.
16. Pour quelles corvées aimeriez-vous avoir une bonne? Expliquez.
17. Pourquoi y a-t-il dans la plupart des cuisines un lave-vaisselle plutôt qu'un égouttoir?
18. Votre vaisselle n'a pas été lavée (le lave-vaisselle ne marche pas), le plancher est sale, les lits ne sont pas faits et les enfants vont rester à la maison toute la journée. Qu'allez-vous faire?
19. Que met-on sur la couverture quand le lit est fait?
20. Quand on fait le lit, que met-on entre le matelas et la couverture?

1. Les corvées de ménage ne sont jamais finies.
2. Comment faire un lit.
3. La ménagère moderne.

It is Saturday, and your parents are away for the day. You and your brothers and sisters have agreed to surprise them by cleaning the house, which is still in disarray from a party the night before. Difficulties arise with some of the tasks and a discussion ensues.

Enact this discussion in French.

to see **voir, apercevoir**
to work **travailler**
to store **faire des réserves (de),
    stocker**
to graze **paître, brouter**
to cultivate **cultiver**
to feed **nourrir**
to milk **traire**
to plow **labourer**
to plant **planter**
to dig **bêcher, creuser**
to drive, lead **conduire**
to bark **aboyer**
to hang up the wash **étendre la
    lessive, étendre le linge**
to suggest **faire penser, suggérer**
to take care (of) **s'occuper (de)**
to be used for **servir à**
to portray, depict **représenter**
to spend *(time)* **passer**
to open **ouvrir**
to lean **s'appuyer, se pencher**
to run away, escape **s'échapper**
to get along well (with) **s'entendre
    bien (avec), faire bon ménage
    (avec)**
to surround **entourer**
to like better than, prefer **aimer
    mieux que, préférer**
not to like **ne pas aimer**

customary, usual **habituel
    (habituelle)**
agricultural **agricole**
dirty **sale**
boring **ennuyeux (ennuyeuse)**
healthy **sain(e)**
in the open air **au grand air**

farm **la ferme**
animal **l'animal** *(m.)*, **animaux** *(pl.)*
horse **le cheval, chevaux** *(pl.)*
cow **la vache**
sheep **le mouton**
duck **le canard**
goose **l'oie** *(f.)*
donkey **l'âne** *(m.)*
dog **le chien**
hen **la poule**
chicken **le poulet**
chick **le poussin**
turkey **le dindon** *(male)*, **la dinde**
    (female)
cat **le chat**
stable **l'écurie** *(f.)*
barn **la grange, l'étable** *(f.)*
pond **l'étang** *(m.)*, **la mare**
field **le champ**
fence **la barrière, la clôture**
gate **la porte, la grille**
wall **le mur**
post **le poteau**

stake **le pieu, le piquet**
tractor **le tracteur**
garden tool **l'outil de jardinage** *(m.)*
rake **le râteau**
hoe **la binette**
shovel **la pelle**
sum of farm tools **le matériel
    agricole, le matériel de ferme**
garden **le jardin**
vegetable **le légume**
farmer **le (la) fermier (fermière)**
wife **la femme**
child **l'enfant** *(m. and f.)*
boy **le garçon**
daughter **la fille**
life **la vie**

La vie à la ferme

48

Analyse de l'illustration

1. Combien de personnes y a-t-il sur le dessin et quelles sont-elles?
2. Quels travaux y a-t-il à faire dans une ferme?
3. Où est la vache et que fait-elle?
4. Que fait la femme du fermier?
5. Que fait le fils?
6. À votre avis, que dit la fermière au petit garçon?
7. Cette ferme est-elle grande ou petite? Comment le savez-vous?
8. Où sont les canards et les oies?
9. À quoi servent les barrières que vous apercevez?
10. Où le chat est-il assis? Que fait-il?
11. Quels outils de jardinage peut-on voir et où sont-ils?
12. Où a-t-on planté les légumes?
13. À quoi les outils de jardinage ont-ils servi?
14. Pourquoi le chien est-il en train d'aboyer?
15. Où sont les poules et où sont les dindes?
16. Si les deux portes étaient ouvertes, quels animaux s'échapperaient sans aucun doute? Où iraient-ils?
17. Que dit le cheval au mouton à votre avis?
18. Qu'est-ce qui vous fait penser que ce dessin représente une ferme européenne?

Points de départ

19. Quelle est la différence entre une écurie et une étable?
20. En général, quels sont les animaux de ferme qui s'entendent bien? Quels sont ceux qui ne s'entendent pas?

Sujets de discussion

1. Avantages et inconvénients de la vie à la ferme.
2. Description d'une grande ferme.
3. Pourquoi j'aimerais (je n'aimerais pas) passer mes vacances d'été dans une ferme.

★ ★

Imaginons et discutons!

Imagine that all the animals in the illustration on the preceding page can talk. What would they say to one another?

Enact this discussion in French.

★

to sit **être assis**
to see **voir**
to visit **visiter**
to get close to **s'approcher de**
to take a picture **prendre une photo**
to eat **manger**
to drink **boire**
to feed **nourrir**
to protect **protéger**
to climb **grimper**
to escape **s'échapper**
to raise, lift **soulever**
to inhabit **habiter**
to hold **tenir**

ferocious **féroce**
dangerous **dangereux (dangereuse)**
carnivorous **carnivore**
herbivorous **herbivore**
inhuman **inhumain(e)**
around **autour de**
many **beaucoup (de), nombreux
    (nombreuses)**

zoo **le zoo**	gazelle **la gazelle**
cage **la cage**	alligator **l'alligator** *(m.)*
animal **l'animal** *(m.)*, **les animaux**	snake **le serpent**
(pl.)	reptile **le reptile**
beast **la bête**	balloon **le ballon**
deer **le cerf**	camera **l'appareil** *(m.)* **photo**
fox **le renard**	railing **le garde-fou, la barrière**
camel **le chameau**	fountain **la fontaine**
leopard **le léopard**	bench **le banc**
panther **la panthère**	sign **la pancarte**
zebra **le zèbre**	ditch **la tranchée, le fossé**
hippopotamus **l'hippopotame** *(m.)*	hill **la colline**
rhinoceros **le rhinocéros**	banana **la banane**
monkey **le singe**	banana peel **la peau de banane**
bear **l'ours** *(m.)*	meat **la viande**
lion **le lion**	popcorn **le pop-corn**
tiger **le tigre**	human being **l'être** *(m.)* **humain**
elephant **l'éléphant** *(m.)*	king **le roi**
gorilla **le gorille**	
giraffe **la girafe**	
wolf **le loup**	
hyena **la hyène**	
antelope **l'antilope** *(f.)*	

Au zoo

49

Analyse de l'illustration

1. Où est le singe et que fait-il?
2. Que mangent les singes? Comment le savez-vous?
3. Quelle personne a un appareil photographique et que fait-elle?
4. Où est le petit garçon? Que tient-il à la main?
5. Pourquoi est-il soulevé par son père?
6. Où la personne est-elle assise?
7. Quelles bêtes sauvages sont en liberté? Où sont-elles?
8. Nommez tous les animaux que vous connaissez et qui ne sont pas sur le dessin.
9. Où doit-il y avoir un fossé?
10. Qui mange du pop-corn?
11. À votre avis, quel animal habite sur la colline?
12. On dirait que le petit garçon au premier plan est en train de dire quelque chose à quelqu'un. Que peut-il dire et à qui?

Points de départ

13. Qui est le «roi des animaux»?
14. Quelle pancarte voit-on généralement dans un zoo?
15. Quels sont les animaux qui mangent de la viande et quels sont ceux qui n'en mangent pas?
16. Décrivez un zoo que vous avez visité.
17. Pourquoi y a-t-il un garde-fou autour de nombreuses cages dans un zoo?
18. Que feriez-vous si vous étiez au zoo et qu'un loup s'échappe de sa cage?
19. Qu'a dit la girafe au gorille?
20. Quelle est la différence entre un être humain et un gorille?

Sujets de discussion

1. Pour ou contre les zoos.
2. Un jour au zoo.
3. Animaux carnivores et animaux herbivores.

Imaginons et discutons!

In the illustration on the preceding page, imagine that the boy with the balloon, the woman with the camera, and the man and little boy at the fountain are a family. They are all having a good time, but they can't agree on what to do, where to go, and which animals to see next.

Enact the scene in French.

to be hot *(of weather)* **faire chaud**
to be cold *(of weather)* **faire froid**
it is sunny **il fait du soleil**
to portray, depict **représenter**
to shine **briller**
to snow **neiger**
to freeze **geler**
to melt **fondre**
to rain **pleuvoir**
to fall **tomber**
to garden **jardiner**
to plant **planter**
to rake **ratisser** *(in a garden)*,
   râteler *(in a field)*
to dig **bêcher, creuser**
to hoe **biner, sarcler**
to sow **semer**
to bloom **fleurir**
to sing **chanter**
to have just *(+ past part.)* **venir de (+**
   inf.)
to wipe **essuyer**
to wipe one's face **s'essuyer la**
   figure
to throw **jeter**
to throw at each other **se jeter**
to forecast **prévoir**
to live **habiter**
to add **additionner, ajouter**
to subtract **soustraire**
to convert **convertir**
to divide **diviser**
to multiply **multiplier**

today's **d'aujourd'hui**
rainy **pluvieux(pluvieuse)**
humid **humide**
cloudy **nuageux (nuageuse)**
foggy **brumeux (brumeuse)**
sunny **ensoleillé(e)**
climatic **climatique**
frozen **gelé(e), glacé(e)**
to the left **à gauche**

weather **le temps**
climate **le climat**
season **la saison**
spring **le printemps**
summer **l'été** *(m.)*
fall **l'automne** *(m.)*
winter **l'hiver** *(m.)*
rain **la pluie**
rain drop **la goutte de pluie**
rainbow **l'arc-en-ciel** *(m.)*
snow **la neige**
snowball **la boule de neige**
water **l'eau** *(f.)*
ice **la glace**
sun **le soleil**
cloud **le nuage**
wind **le vent**
hail **la grêle**
thunder **le tonnerre**
lightning **l'éclair** *(m.)*, **la foudre**
storm *(rain, wind, or snow)*
   la tempête
hurricane **l'ouragan** *(m.)*

tornado **la tornade**
seed **la graine**
tulip **la tulipe**
tree **l'arbre** *(m.)*
leaf **la feuille**
(garden) rake **le râteau**
(garden) hoe **la binette**
furrow **le sillon**
bird **l'oiseau** *(m.)*
face **la figure, le visage**
ice cream **la glace, la crème glacée**
region **la région**
equivalent **l'équivalent** *(m.)*
temperature **la température**
degree **le degré**
centigrade **le centigrade (le degré**
   Celsius)
zero **zéro**
water vapor **la vapeur d'eau**

freezing point **le point de**
   congélation (32° Fahrenheit =
   0° Celsius) (Pour convertir les
   degrés Celsius en degrés
   Fahrenheit, il faut multiplier
   par 9, diviser par 5 et
   additionner 32. Pour convertir
   les degrés Fahrenheit en degrés
   Celsius, il faut soustraire 32,
   multiplier par 5 et diviser
   par 9.)

Les saisons

50

Analyse de l'illustration

1. Comment savez-vous que le dessin à gauche représente le printemps?
2. Que fait le monsieur avec la binette?
3. Sur le même dessin, que fait la dame?
4. Qui vient d'acheter une glace?
5. Pourquoi est-ce que le monsieur s'essuie la figure?
6. Quel dessin représente l'automne? Comment le savez-vous?
7. Que font les garçons dans la neige?

Points de départ

8. Quel temps fait-il en été dans votre région? et en hiver?
9. En quelle saison les tulipes fleurissent-elles?
10. Quel est le point de congélation?
11. Quand doit-on planter des graines?
12. Décrivez le climat là où vous habitez.
13. Quand voit-on un arc-en-ciel?
14. Quand la neige fond-elle?
15. Quand la température est de 95° Fahrenheit, quelle est-elle en degrés Celsius?
16. Quand la température est de 25° Celsius, quel est l'équivalent en degrés Fahrenheit?
17. Quelle est la température en ce moment, à peu près, en degrés Fahrenheit et en degrés Celsius?
18. Décrivez le temps d'aujourd'hui.
19. Prévoyez le temps pour demain.
20. Décrivez les différences entre l'hiver et l'été.

Sujets de discussion

1. La saison que je préfère.
2. Jardiner au printemps.
3. Différents climats aux États-Unis.

Imaginons et discutons!

The weather is terrible! More than half your French class is absent, but there you are with some of your classmates. Naturally, the conversation turns to the weather. Take your time because your teacher is absent too.

Enact this situation in French.

to be born **naître, être né(e)**
to live **vivre; habiter**
to die **mourir**
to get married **se marier**
to marry *(tr.)* **épouser, se marier**
    avec
to age, grow old **vieillir**
to pray **prier**
to weep, cry **pleurer**
to forget **oublier**
to rain **pleuvoir**
to represent, portray **représenter**
to hold **tenir**
to attend **assister (à)**
to sing **chanter**
to suspend **suspendre**
to console oneself **se consoler**
to happen **arriver**

single **célibataire**
married **marié(e)**
young **jeune**
old **vieux (vieil) (vieille)**
happy **heureux (heureuse)**
sad **triste**
deceased **défunt(e)**
next to **près de**

cycle **le cycle**
life **la vie**
birth **la naissance**
death **la mort**
youth **la jeunesse**
old age **la vieillesse**
happiness **le bonheur**
unhappiness **le malheur**
husband **le mari, l'époux**
wife **la femme, l'épouse**
father **le père, le papa**
mother **la mère, la maman**
baby **le bébé**
marriage **le mariage**
celibacy **le célibat**
(married) couple **le couple (marié)**
divorce **le divorce**
wedding **le mariage, les noces**
wedding day **le jour du mariage**
bride **la mariée**
groom **le marié**
newlyweds **les jeunes mariés**
wedding ring **l'alliance** *(f.)*

honeymoon (wedding trip) **la lune de miel (le voyage de noces)**
bedroom **la chambre**
best man **le garçon d'honneur**
bridesmaid, maid of honor **la demoiselle d'honneur**
Catholic **le (la) catholique**
Protestant **le (la) protestant(e)**
Jew **le (la) juif (juive)**
church **l'église** *(f.)*
temple *(Jewish)* **la synagogue**
priest **le prêtre**
rabbi **le rabbin** *(no fem.:* **elle est rabbin)**
minister, pastor **le pasteur** *(no fem.:* **elle est pasteur)**
widower **le veuf**
widow **la veuve**
cemetery, graveyard **le cimetière**
burial **l'enterrement** *(m.)*
funeral **les obsèques** *(f.)*
coffin **le cercueil**
grave **la tombe**

tombstone **la pierre tombale**
mourners **le cortège funèbre**
umbrella **le parapluie**
fire **le feu**
in the presence of **en présence de**
candle **le cierge**
vers **le vers**
poet **le poète**
flight **le vol**
course **le cours**

Le cycle de la vie

51

1. Pourquoi cette jeune femme a-t-elle l'air si heureuse?
2. Où se trouve-t-elle?
3. Pourquoi les mariés sont-ils en présence d'un pasteur?
4. Ce mariage a-t-il lieu dans une église catholique, protestante ou dans une synagogue? Comment le savez-vous?
5. Décrivez l'expression des deux personnes âgées.
6. Dans quelle image pleut-il?
7. Où est le défunt?
8. Pourquoi l'image de l'enterrement est-elle triste?
9. Quelles sont les quatre parties du cycle de la vie représentées par les quatre images?

Points de départ

10. Où êtes-vous né(e) et où avez-vous passé la plus grande partie de votre jeunesse?
11. Qu'est-ce qu'une lune de miel?
12. Qu'arriverait-il si le jour du mariage le marié oubliait l'alliance?
13. Quelle est votre définition du bonheur?
14. Si vous êtes marié(e), décrivez votre mariage. Sinon, pourquoi n'êtes-vous pas marié(e)?
15. Que préféreriez-vous: passer votre lune de miel chez vous ou faire un voyage de noces?
16. Qu'est-ce qu'un(e) veuf (veuve)?
17. Que fait-on (et que ne fait-on pas) dans une église ou dans une synagogue?
18. Qu'est-ce qu'un cimetière?
19. À quoi sert une pierre tombale?
20. Qui assiste généralement à un mariage traditionnel?

Sujets de discussion

1. L'histoire de la vie d'un couple de personnes âgées.
2. Mariage ou célibat.
3. Le divorce.

**Imaginons et
discutons!**

Alphonse de Lamartire, a famous French poet, once wrote: «O temps, suspends ton vol! Et vous, heures propices, suspendez votre cours!» You and a group of friends exchange thoughts about the present stage of your lives and your hopes for the future.

Enact this discussion in French.

to border (on) **être limitrophe de**
to have in common **avoir en commun**
to choose, elect **choisir, élire**
to govern, rule **gouverner, diriger**
to earn *(money)* **gagner**
to spend *(money)* **dépenser**
to form part of **faire partie de**
to save **sauver**
to export **exporter**
to harvest **récolter**
to separate **séparer**

transatlantic **transatlantique**
only, just **seulement**
own **propre**
near, close (to) **proche (de), près (de)**
quite close (to) **tout près (de)**
several **plusieurs**
red **rouge**
white **blanc (blanche)**
chief, most important **principal(e)**
famous **célèbre, très connu(e)**

north **le nord**
northwest **le nord-ouest**
northeast **le nord-est**
south **le sud**
southwest **le sud-ouest**
southeast **le sud-est**
east **l'est** *(m.)*
west **l'ouest** *(m.)*

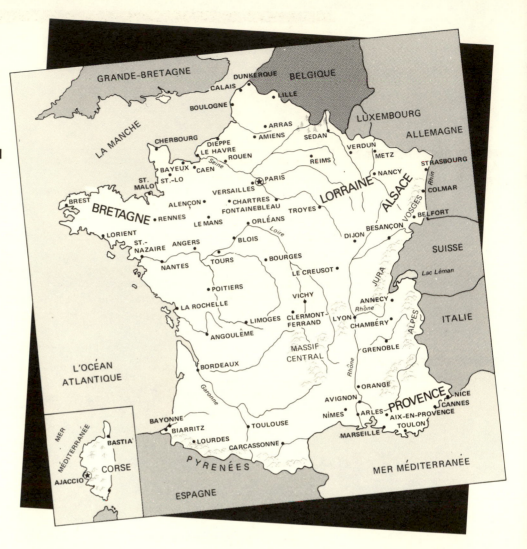

map **la carte**
location **la position, l'endroit** *(m.)*
geography **la géographie**
crossing **la traversée**
center **le centre**
crossroads **le carrefour**
border **la frontière**
city **la ville**
province **la province**
department *(administrative division of French territory)* **le département**
country, nation **le pays, nation**
capital **la capitale**
republic **la république**
democracy **la démocratie**
monarchy **la monarchie**
dictatorship **la dictature**
communism **le communisme**
fascism **le fascisme**
proletariat *(class)* **le prolétariat**
government **le gouvernement**
form of government **la forme de gouvernement**
law **la loi**
constitution **la constitution**
parliament **le parlement**
senate **le sénat**

house of representatives **la chambre des députés**
president **le (la) président(e)**
prime minister **le premier ministre** *(no fem.:* **elle est premier ministre**)
head of state **le chef d'État** *(no fem.:* **elle est chef d'État**)
king **le roi**
queen **la reine**
mountain **la montagne**
(mountain) chain **la chaîne (de montagne)**
river **la rivière**
island **l'île** *(f.)*
port **le port**
coast, shore **la côte**
coastline **le littoral**
industry **l'industrie** *(f.)*
trade, commerce **le commerce**
money **l'argent** *(m.)*
language **la langue**
France **la France**
Frenchman, Frenchwoman **le (la) Français(e)**
United States of America, U.S.A. **les États-Unis d'Amérique**
Switzerland **la Suisse**

Luxembourg **le Luxembourg**
Canada **le Canada**
Canadian *(inhabitants)* **le (la) Canadien (Canadienne)**
American *(inhabitants)* **l'Américain(e)**
England **l'Angleterre**
English *(inhabitants)* **l'Anglais(e)**
inhabitant of Paris **le (la) Parisien (Parisienne)**
inhabitant of Bordeaux **le (la) Bordelais(e)**
inhabitant of Lyon **le (la) Lyonnais(e)**
inhabitant of Marseilles **le (la) Marseillais(e)**
Provence *(region)* **la Provence**
inhabitant of Provence **le (la) Provençal(e)**
language of Provence **le provençal**
Mediterranean Sea **la mer Méditerranée**
Lorraine **la Lorraine**
Riviera **la Côte d'Azur**
Alsace **l'Alsace** *(f.)*
castle **le château**
wine **le vin**
occupation **l'occupation** *(f.)*
rule, domination **la domination**
siege **le siège**

La carte de France

52

Analyse de l'illustration

1. Décrivez la position des deux provinces suivantes: L'Alsace et la Bretagne.
2. Quelle est la capitale de la France? Où se trouve-t-elle?
3. Sur quelles rivières la ville de Lyon se trouve-t-elle?
4. Que sont les Pyrénées et où sont-elles?
5. Quel est le pays limitrophe de la France au nord-est?
6. Nommez deux ports importants pour le commerce transatlantique. Où se trouvent-ils?
7. Quelle est la ville française la plus proche de l'Angleterre? Décrivez sa position.
8. Décrivez la position de Marseille.
9. Pourquoi la Corse est-elle célèbre? Où se trouve-t-elle?
10. Nommez un lac situé en France et en Suisse et expliquez quelle partie est française et quelle partie est suisse.
11. Comme «le sud» aux États-Unis, la Provence est seulement une région; ce n'est pas un département. Nommez plusieurs villes de cette région. Que savez-vous sur chacune d'elles?
12. Que savez-vous sur Versailles? Où est-ce?

Points de départ

13. Dans quels autres pays parle-t-on français?
14. Quelle est la forme du gouvernement en France?
15. Qu'est-ce qu'une démocratie? Qu'est-ce qu'une monarchie?
16. Expliquez ce qu'est une dictature. Donnez des exemples.
17. Qu'est-ce que le communisme?
18. L'Alsace et la Lorraine ont-elles toujours été françaises? Que savez-vous sur ces provinces?
19. Pourquoi la Loire est-elle un fleuve célèbre?
20. Pourquoi la région de Bordeaux est-elle très connue?

Sujets de discussion

1. Les régions de France.
2. Formes de gouvernement en Europe.
3. La situation stratégique de la France.

Imaginons et discutons!

You and a group of friends are going to take a trip together to France. Since part of the fun of a trip is planning it, you and your friends can begin enjoying yourselves right now. Each one should say where he or she wants to go and why.

Enact this discussion in French.

Appendice

Auxiliary Verbs (Verbes Auxiliaires)

avoir *to have*		**être** *to be*	

PRESENT PARTICIPLE (PARTICIPE PRÉSENT)

ayant *having* **étant** *being*

PAST PARTICIPLE (PARTICIPE PASSÉ)

eu *had* **été** *been*

PRESENT INDICATIVE (PRÉSENT DE L'INDICATIF)

I have		*I am*	
j'**ai**	nous **avons**	je **suis**	nous **sommes**
tu **as**	vous **avez**	tu **es**	vous **êtes**
il **a**	ils **ont**	il **est**	ils **sont**

IMPERFECT INDICATIVE (IMPARFAIT DE L'INDICATIF)

I had, used to have		*I was, used to be*	
j'**avais**	nous **avions**	j'**étais**	nous **étions**
tu **avais**	vous **aviez**	tu **étais**	vous **étiez**
il **avait**	ils **avaient**	il **était**	ils **étaient**

SIMPLE PAST (PASSÉ SIMPLE)

I had		*I was*	
j'**eus**	nous **eûmes**	je **fus**	nous **fûmes**
tu **eus**	vous **eûtes**	tu **fus**	vous **fûtes**
il **eut**	ils **eurent**	il **fut**	ils **furent**

FUTURE (FUTUR)

I will have		*I will be*	
j'**aurai**	nous **aurons**	je **serai**	nous **serons**
tu **auras**	vous **aurez**	tu **seras**	vous **serez**
il **aura**	ils **auront**	il **sera**	ils **seront**

CONDITIONAL (CONDITIONNEL)

I would have		*I would be*	
j'**aurais**	nous **aurions**	je **serais**	nous **serions**
tu **aurais**	vous **auriez**	tu **serais**	vous **seriez**
il **aurait**	ils **auraient**	il **serait**	ils **seraient**

PRESENT SUBJUNCTIVE (PRÉSENT DU SUBJONCTIF)

(that) I have, may have		*(that) I am, may be*	
(que) j'**aie**	(que) nous **ayons**	(que) je **sois**	(que) nous **soyons**
(que) tu **aies**	(que) vous **ayez**	(que) tu **sois**	(que) vous **soyez**
(qu')il **ait**	(qu')ils **aient**	(qu')il **soit**	(qu')ils **soient**

IMPERATIVE (IMPÉRATIF)

aie *have* **sois** *be*
ayons *let us have* **soyons** *let us be*
ayez *have* **soyez** *be*

COMPOUND PAST (PASSÉ COMPOSÉ)

I have had, had

j'**ai eu**	nous **avons eu**
tu **as eu**	vous **avez eu**
il **a eu**	ils **ont eu**

I have been, was

j'**ai été**	nous **avons été**
tu **as été**	vous **avez été**
il **a été**	ils **ont été**

PLUPERFECT (PLUS-QUE-PARFAIT)

I had had

j'**avais eu**, etc.

I had been

j'**avais été**, etc.

PAST ANTERIOR (PASSÉ ANTÉRIEUR)

I had had

j'**eus eu**, etc.

I had been

j'**eus été**, etc.

FUTURE PERFECT (FUTUR ANTÉRIEUR)

I will have had

j'**aurai eu**	nous **aurons eu**
tu **auras eu**	vous **aurez eu**
il **aura eu**	ils **auront eu**

I will have been

j'**aurai été**	nous **aurons été**
tu **auras été**	vous **aurez été**
il **aura été**	ils **auront été**

PAST CONDITIONAL (CONDITIONNEL PASSÉ)

I would have had

j'**aurais eu**, etc.

I would have been

j'**aurais été**, etc.

PAST SUBJUNCTIVE (SUBJONCTIF PASSÉ)

(that) I have had, had, may have had

(que) j'**aie eu**, etc.

(that) I have been, was, may have been

(que) j'**aie été**, etc.

Regular Verbs (Verbes Réguliers)

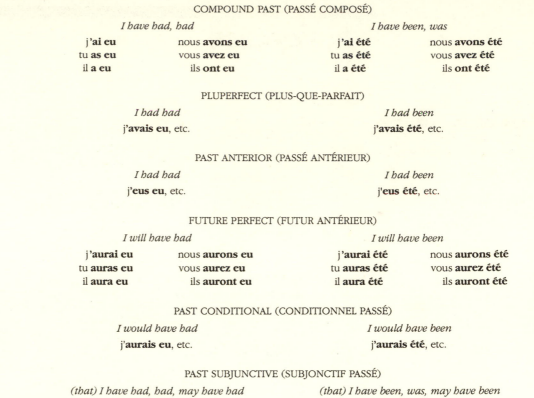

-er		-ir		-re	
parler	*to speak*	**finir**	*to finish*	**vendre**	*to sell*
parlant	*speaking*	**finissant**	*finishing*	**vendant**	*selling*
parlé	*spoken*	**fini**	*finished*	**vendu**	*sold*

PRESENT INDICATIVE (PRÉSENT DE L'INDICATIF)

I speak, am speaking	*I finish, am finishing*	*I sell, am selling*
je **parle**	je **finis**	je **vends**
tu **parles**	tu **finis**	tu **vends**
il **parle**	il **finit**	il **vend**
nous **parlons**	nous **finissons**	nous **vendons**
vous **parlez**	vous **finissez**	vous **vendez**
ils **parlent**	ils **finissent**	ils **vendent**

IMPERFECT INDICATIVE (IMPARFAIT DE L'INDICATIF)

I was speaking, used to speak, spoke	*I was finishing, used to finish, finished*	*I was selling, used to sell, sold*
je **parlais**	je **finissais**	je **vendais**
tu **parlais**	tu **finissais**	tu **vendais**
il **parlait**	il **finissait**	il **vendait**
nous **parlions**	nous **finissions**	nous **vendions**
vous **parliez**	vous **finissiez**	vous **vendiez**
ils **parlaient**	ils **finissaient**	ils **vendaient**

SIMPLE PAST (PASSÉ SIMPLE)

I spoke	*I finished*	*I sold*
je **parlai**	je **finis**	je **vendis**
tu **parlas**	tu **finis**	tu **vendis**
il **parla**	il **finit**	il **vendit**
nous **parlâmes**	nous **finîmes**	nous **vendîmes**
vous **parlâtes**	vous **finîtes**	vous **vendîtes**
ils **parlèrent**	ils **finirent**	ils **vendirent**

FUTURE (FUTUR)

I will speak	*I will finish*	*I will sell*
je **parlerai**	je **finirai**	je **vendrai**
tu **parleras**	tu **finiras**	tu **vendras**
il **parlera**	il **finira**	il **vendra**
nous **parlerons**	nous **finirons**	nous **vendrons**
vous **parlerez**	vous **finirez**	vous **vendrez**
ils **pareleront**	ils **finiront**	ils **vendront**

CONDITIONAL (CONDITIONNEL)

I would speak	*I would finish*	*I would sell*
je **parlerais**	je **finirais**	je **vendrais**
tu **parlerais**	tu **finirais**	tu **vendrais**
il **parlerait**	il **finirait**	il **vendrait**
nous **parlerions**	nous **finirions**	nous **vendrions**
vous **parleriez**	vous **finiriez**	vous **vendriez**
ils **parleraient**	ils **finiraient**	ils **vendraient**

PRESENT SUBJUNCTIVE (SUBJONCTIF PRÉSENT)

(that) I speak, am speaking, may speak	*(that) I finish, am finishing, may finish*	*(that) I sell, am selling, may sell*
(que) je **parle**	(que) je **finisse**	(que) je **vende**
(que) tu **parles**	(que) tu **finisses**	(que) tu **vendes**
(qu')il **parle**	(qu')il **finisse**	(qu')il **vende**
(que) nous **parlions**	(que) nous **finissions**	(que) nous **vendions**
(que) vous **parliez**	(que) vous **finissiez**	(que) vous **vendiez**
(qu')ils **parlent**	(qu')ils **finissent**	(qu')ils **vendent**

IMPERATIVE (IMPÉRATIF)

parle	*speak*	**vends**	*sell*	**finis**	*finish*
parlons	*let us speak*	**vendons**	*let us sell*	**finissons**	*let us finish*
parlez	*speak*	**vendez**	*sell*	**finissez**	*finish*

Compound Tenses (Temps composés)

COMPOUND PAST (PASSÉ COMPOSÉ)

I have spoken, spoke	*I have finished, finished*	*I have sold, sold*
j'**ai parlé**	j'**ai fini**	j'**ai vendu**
tu **as parlé**	tu **as fini**	tu **as vendu**
il **a parlé**	il **a fini**	il **a vendu**
nous **avons parlé**	nous **avons fini**	nous **avons vendu**
vous **avez parlé**	vous **avez fini**	vous **avez vendu**
ils **ont parlé**	ils **ont fini**	ils **ont vendu**

PLUPERFECT (PLUS-QUE-PARFAIT)

I had spoken	*I had finished*	*I had sold*
j'**avais parlé**, etc.	j'**avais fini**, etc.	j'**avais vendu**, etc.

PAST ANTERIOR (PASSÉ ANTÉRIEUR)

I had spoken	*I had finished*	*I had sold*
j'**eus parlé**, etc	j'**eus fini**, etc.	j'**eus vendu**, etc.

FUTURE PERFECT (FUTUR ANTÉRIEUR)

I will have spoken	*I will have finished*	*I will have sold*
j'**aurai parlé**	j'**aurai fini**	j'**aurai vendu**
tu **auras parlé**	tu **auras fini**	tu **auras vendu**
il **aura parlé**	il **aura fini**	il **aura vendu**
nous **aurons parlé**	nous **aurons fini**	nous **aurons vendu**
vous **aurez parlé**	vous **aurez fini**	vous **aurez vendu**
ils **auront parlé**	ils **auront fini**	ils **auront vendu**

PAST CONDITIONAL (CONDITIONNEL PASSÉ)

I would have spoken	*I would have finished*	*I would have sold*
j'**aurais parlé**, etc.	j'**aurais fini**, etc.	j'**aurais vendu**, etc.

PAST SUBJUNCTIVE (SUBJONCTIF PASSÉ)

(that) I have spoken, spoke, may have spoken	*(that) I have finished, finished, may have finished*	*(that) I have sold, sold, may have sold*
(que) j'**aie parlé**, etc.	(que) j'**aie fini**, etc.	(que) j'**aie vendu**, etc.

Regular Verbs Conjugated with *être* in the Compound Tenses (Verbes Réguliers Conjugués avec *être* aux Temps Composés)

entrer *to enter*, **entrant** *entering*, **entré** *entered*

COMPOUND PAST (PASSÉ COMPOSÉ)	PAST ANTERIOR (PASSÉ ANTÉRIEUR)	PAST CONDITIONAL (CONDITIONNEL PASSÉ)
je **suis entré(e)**	je **fus entré(e)**, etc.	je **serais entré(e)**, etc.
tu **es entré(e)**		
il **est entré**	FUTURE PERFECT (FUTUR ANTÉRIEUR)	PAST SUBJUNCTIVE (SUBJONCTIF PASSÉ)
elle **est entrée**		
nous **sommes entré(e)s**	je **serai entré(e)**	(que) je **sois entré(e)**, etc.
vous **êtes entré(e)s**	tu **seras entré(e)**	
ils **sont entrés**	il **sera entré**	
elles sont **entrées**	elle **sera entrée**	
	nous **serons entré(e)s**	
PLUPERFECT (PLUS-QUE-PARFAIT)	vous **serez entré(e)s**	
	ils **seront entrés**	
j'**étais entré(e)**, etc.	elles **seront entrées**	

Irregular Verbs (Verbes Irréguliers)

Full endings for the future tense are:

je	-ai	**nous**	-ons
tu	-as	**vous**	-ez
il	-a	**ils**	-ont

Full endings for the imperfect and conditional are:

je	-ais	**nous**	-ions
tu	-ais	**vous**	-iez
il	-ait	**ils**	-aient

Infinitives, past participles, stems, and irregular forms appear in **bold** type.

---

acquérir *to acquire*

PRES. IND.	j'**acquiers,** tu acquiers, il acquiert, nous **acquér**ons, vous acquérez, ils acquièrent
PRES. SUBJ.	j'acquière, nous acquérions
FUT. IND.	j'**acquerr**ai, etc.
CONDIT.	j'acquerrais, etc.

aller *to go*

PRES. IND.	je **vais**, tu **vas**[1], il **va**, nous **all**ons, vous allez, ils **vont**
FUT. IND..	j'**ir**ai, etc.
CONDIT.	j'**ir**ais, etc.
PRES. SUBJ.	j'**aill**e, tu ailles, il aille, nous **all**ions, vous alliez, ils **aill**ent
PASSÉ COMP.	je suis **allé(e)**, etc.
PASSÉ SIMP.	il alla, ils allèrent[2]
IMPERF.	j'**all**ais, etc.
PRES. PART.	allant

s'en aller *to go away, like* **aller**

PRES. IND.	je m'en vais, tu t'en vas, il s'en va, nous nous en allons, vous vous en allez, ils s'en vont
PASSÉ COMP.	je me suis en **allé(e)**, etc.

s'apercevoir *to notice, like* **recevoir**

PRES. IND.	je m'aper**çois**, tu t'aperçois, il s'aperçoit, nous nous aper**cev**ons, vous vous apercevez, ils s'aper**çoiv**ent
PASSÉ COMP.	je me suis **aperçu(e)**, etc.

s'asseoir *to sit down*

PRES. IND.	je m'**assie**ds, tu t'assieds, il s'assied, nous nous **assey**ons, vous vous asseyez, ils s'asseyent
FUT. IND.	je m'**assié**rai, etc.
CONDIT.	je m'**assié**rais, etc.
PRES. SUBJ.	je m'**assey**e, tu t'asseyes, il s'asseye, nous nous asseyons, vous vous asseyez, ils s'asseyent
PASSÉ COMP.	je me suis **assis(e)**, etc.
PASSÉ SIMP.	il s'assit, ils s'assirent
IMPERF.	je m'**assey**ais, etc.
PRES. PART.	(s')asseyant

atteindre *to attain, like* **craindre**

PRES. IND.	j'att**eins**, tu atteins, il atteint, nous att**eign**ons, vous atteignez, ils atteignent
PASSÉ COMP.	j'ai **atteint**, etc.

battre *to beat, like* **vendre,** *but with* **t** *in present tense and stem*

PRES. IND.	je **bat**s, tu bats, il bat, nous **batt**ons, vous battez, ils battent
PASSÉ COMP.	j'ai **battu**, etc.

boire *to drink*

PRES. IND.	je **boi**s, tu bois, il bois, nous **buv**ons, vous buvez, ils **boiv**ent
PRES. SUBJ.	je **boiv**e, tu boives, il boive, nous **buv**ions, vous buviez, ils **boiv**ent
FUT.	je **boir**ai, etc.
CONDIT.	je **boir**ais, etc.
PASSÉ COMP.	j'ai **bu**, etc.
PASSÉ SIMP.	il but, ils burent
IMPERF.	je **buv**ais, etc.
PRES. PART.	buvant

conduire *to drive*

PRES. IND.	je **condui**s, tu conduis, il conduit, nous **conduis**ons, vous conduisez, ils conduisent
PRES. SUBJ.	je **conduis**e, tu conduises, il conduise, nous conduisions, vous conduisiez, ils conduisent
FUT.	je **conduir**ai, etc.
CONDIT.	je **conduir**ais, etc.

1. Familiar imperative: **va,** except when followed by **y: Vas-y** *Go there.*
2. Regular **passé simple** for **-er** verbs.

111

PASSÉ COMP.	j'ai **conduit**, etc.
PASSÉ SIMP.	il **conduisit**, ils conduisirent
IMPERF.	je **conduis**ais, etc.
PRES. PART.	conduisant

connaître *to know*

PRES. IND.	je **connais**, tu connais, il connaît, nous **connaiss**ons, vous connaissez, ils connaissent
PRES. SUBJ.	je **connaiss**e, tu connaisses, il connaisse, nous connaissions, vous connaissiez, ils connaissent
FUT.	je **connaîtr**ai, etc.
CONDIT.	je **connaîtr**ais, etc.
PASSÉ COMP.	j'ai **connu**, etc.
PASSÉ SIMP.	il connut, ils connurent
IMPERF.	je **connaiss**ais, etc.
PRES. PART.	connaissant

construire *to build, like* **conduire**

| PRES. IND. | je con**struis**, tu construis, il construit, nous con**strui**sons, vous construisez, ils construisent |
| PASSÉ COMP. | j'ai **construit**, etc. |

coudre *to sew*

PRES. IND.	je **cou**ds, tu couds, il coud, nous **cous**ons, vous cousez, ils cousent
PRES. SUBJ.	je **cous**e, tu couses, il couse, nous **cous**ions, vous cousiez, ils cousent
FUT.	je **coudr**ai, etc.
CONDIT.	je **coudr**ais, etc.
PASSÉ COMP.	j'ai **cousu**, etc.
PASSÉ SIMP.	il **cousit**, ils cousirent
IMPERF.	je **cous**ais, etc.
PRES. PART.	cousant

courir *to run*

PRES. IND.	je **cour**s, tu cours, il court, nous courons, vous courez, ils courent
PRES. SUBJ.	je **cour**e, tu coures, il coure, nous courions, vous couriez, ils courent
FUT.	je **courr**ai, etc.
CONDIT.	je **courr**ais, etc.
PASSÉ COMP.	j'ai **couru**, etc.
PASSÉ SIMP.	il **courut**, ils coururent
IMPERF.	je **cour**ais, etc.
PRES. PART.	courant

couvrir *to cover, like* **ouvrir**

| PRES. IND. | je **couvr**e, tu couvres, il couvre, nous couvrons, vous couvrez, ils couvrent |
| PASSÉ COMP. | j'ai **couvert**, etc. |

craindre *to fear*

PRES. IND.	je **crain**s, tu crains, il craint, nous **craign**ons, vous craignez, ils craignent
PRES. SUBJ.	je **craign**e, tu craignes, il craigne, nous craignions, vous craigniez, ils craignent
FUT.	je **craindr**ai, etc.
CONDIT.	je **craindr**ais, etc.
PASSÉ COMP.	j'ai **craint**, etc.
PASSÉ SIMP.	il **craignit**, ils craignirent
IMPERF.	je **craign**ais, etc.
PRES. PART.	craignant

croire *to believe*

PRES. IND.	je **crois**, tu crois, il croit, nous croyons, vous **croy**ez, ils **croi**ent
PRES. SUBJ.	je **croi**e, tu croies, il croie, nous **croy**ions, vous croyiez, ils **croi**ent
FUT.	je **croir**ai, etc.
CONDIT.	je **croir**ais, etc.

PASSÉ COMP.	j'ai **cru**, etc.
PASSÉ SIMP.	il **crut**, ils crurent
IMPERF.	je **croy**ais, etc.
PRES. PART.	croyant

cueillir *to pick, gather*

PRES. IND.	je **cueille**, tu cueilles, il cueille, nous cueillons, vous cueillez, ils cueillent
FUT.	je **cueiller**ai, etc.
CONDIT.	je **cueiller**ais, etc.
PASSÉ COMP.	j'ai **cueilli**, etc.

cuire, *like* conduire

| PRES. IND. | je **cuis**, tu cuis, il cuit, nous **cuis**ons, vous cuisez, ils cuisent |
| PASSÉ COMP. | j'ai **cuit**, etc. |

devoir *to owe; to have to*

PRES. IND.	je **dois**, tu dois, il doit, nous **dev**ons, vous devez, ils **doiv**ent
PRES. SUBJ.	je **doiv**e, tu doives, il doive, nous **dev**ions, vous deviez, ils **doiv**ent
FUT.	je **devr**ai, etc.
CONDIT.	je **devr**ais, etc.
PASSÉ COMP.	j'ai **dû**, etc.
PASSÉ SIMP.	il **dut**, ils durent
IMPERF.	je **dev**ais, etc.
PRES. PART.	devant

dire *to say*

PRES. IND.	je **dis**, tu dis, il dit, nous **dis**ons, vous **dites**, ils disent
PRES. SUBJ.	je **dis**e, tu dises, il dise, nous disions, vous disiez, ils disent
FUT.	je **dir**ai, etc.
CONDIT.	je **dir**ais, etc.
PASSÉ COMP.	j'ai **dit**, etc.
PASSÉ SIMP.	il **dit**, ils dirent
IMPERF.	je **dis**ais, etc.
PRES. PART.	disant

dormir *to sleep, like* partir

| PRES. IND. | je **dors**, tu dors, il dort, nous **dorm**ons, vous dormez, ils dorment |
| PASSÉ COMP. | j'ai **dormi**, etc. |

écrire *to write*

PRES. IND.	j'**écris**, tu écris, il écrit, nous **écriv**ons, vous écrivez, ils écrivent
PRES. SUBJ.	j'**écriv**e, tu écrives, il écrive, nous écrivions, vous écriviez, ils écrivent
FUT.	j'**écrir**ai, etc.
CONDIT.	j'**écrir**ais, etc.
PASSÉ COMP.	j'ai **écrit**, etc.
PASSÉ SIMP.	il **écrivit**, ils écrivirent
IMPERF.	j'**écriv**ais, etc.
PRES. PART.	écrivant

envoyer *to send*

FUT.	j'**enverr**ai, etc.
CONDIT.	j'**enverr**ais, etc.
Otherwise a regular **-yer** verb	

éteindre *to extinguish, like* craindre

| PRES. IND. | j'**éteins**, tu éteins, il éteint, nous **éteign**ons, vous éteignez, ils éteignent |
| PASSÉ COMP. | j'ai **éteint**, etc. |

faire *to do, make*

PRES. IND.	je **fai**s, tu fais, il fait, nous **fais**ons, vous **faites**, ils **font**
PRES. SUBJ.	je **fasse**, tu fasses, il fasse, nous fassions, vous fassiez, ils fassent
FUT.	je **fer**ai, etc.
CONDIT.	je **fer**ais, etc.
PASSÉ COMP.	j'ai **fait**, etc.
PASSÉ SIMP.	il **fit**, ils firent
IMPERF.	je **fais**ais, etc.
PRES. PART.	faisant

falloir *to have to, must (impersonal)*

PRES. IND.	il **faut**
PRES. SUBJ.	il **faille**
FUT.	il **faudr**a
CONDIT.	il **faudr**ait
PASSÉ COMP.	il a **fall**u
PASSÉ SIMP.	il fallut
IMPERF.	il **fall**ait

fuir *to flee*

PRES. IND.	je **fui**s, tu fuis, il fuit, nous **fuy**ons, vous fuyez, ils **fui**ent
PRES. SUBJ.	je **fui**e, tu fuies, il fuie, nous **fuy**ions, vous fuyiez, ils **fui**ent
FUT.	je **fuir**ai, etc.
CONDIT.	je **fuir**ais, etc.
PASSÉ COMP.	j'ai **fui**, etc.
PASSÉ SIMP.	je fuis, ils fuirent
IMPERF.	je **fuy**ais, etc.
PRES. PART.	fuyant

haïr *to hate*

PRES. IND.	je hais, tu hais, il hait, nous **haïss**ons, vous haïssez, ils haïssent
PRES. SUBJ.	je **haïss**e, tu haïsses, il haïsse, nous haïssions, vous haïssiez, ils haïssent
FUT.	je **haïr**ai, etc.
CONDIT.	je **haïr**ais, etc.
PASSÉ COMP.	j'ai **haï**, etc.
PASSÉ SIMP.	je haïs, ils haïrent
IMPERF.	je **haïss**ais, etc.
PRES. PART.	haïssant

s'inscrire *to enroll, like* **écrire**

PRES. IND.	je m'**inscri**s, tu t'inscris, il s'inscrit, nous nous **inscriv**ons, vous vous inscrivez, ils s'inscrivent
PASSÉ COMP.	je me suis **inscrit(e)**, etc.

lire *to read*

PRES. IND.	je **li**s, tu lis, il lit, nous **lis**ons, vous lisez, ils lisent
PRES. SUBJ.	je **lis**e, tu lises, il lise, nous lisions, vous lisiez, ils lisent
FUT.	je **lir**ai, etc.
CONDIT.	je **lir**ais, etc.
PASSÉ COMP.	j'ai **lu**, etc.
PASSÉ SIMP.	il lut, ils lurent
IMPERF.	je **lis**ais, etc.
PRES. PART.	lisant

mentir *to lie, like* **partir**

PRES. IND.	je **men**s, tu mens, il ment, nous **ment**ons, vous mentez, ils mentent
PASSÉ COMP.	j'ai **menti**, etc.

mettre *to put*

PRES. IND.	je **met**s, tu mets, il met, nous **mett**ons, vous mettez, ils mettent
PRES. SUBJ.	je **mett**e, tu mettes, il mette, nous mettions, vous mettiez, ils mettent
FUT.	je **mettr**ai, etc.
CONDIT.	je **mettr**ais, etc.
PASSÉ COMP.	j'ai **mis**, etc.
PASSÉ SIMP.	il mit, ils mirent
IMPERF.	je **mett**ais, etc.
PRES. PART.	mettant

mordre *to bite, like* **vendre**

PRES. IND.	je **mord**s, tu mords, il mord, nous **mord**ons, vous **mord**ez, ils **mord**ent
PASSÉ COMP.	j'ai **mordu**, etc.

mourir *to die*

PRES. IND.	je **meur**s, tu meurs, il meurt, nous **mour**ons, vous mourez, ils **meur**ent
PRES. SUBJ.	je **meur**e, tu meures, il meure, nous **mour**ions, vous mouriez, ils **meur**ent
FUT.	je **mourr**ai, etc.
CONDIT.	je **mourr**ais, etc.
PASSÉ COMP.	je suis **mort**, etc.
PASSÉ SIMP.	il **mourut**, ils moururent
IMPERF.	je **mour**ais, etc.
PRES. PART.	mourant

naître *to be born*

PRES. IND.	je **nai**s, tu nais, il naît, nous **naiss**ons, vous naissez, ils naissent
PRES. SUBJ.	je **naiss**e, tu naisses, il naisse, nous naissions, vous naissiez, ils naissent
FUT.	je **naîtr**ai, etc.
CONDIT.	je **naîtr**ais, etc.
PASSÉ COMP.	je suis **né(e)**, etc.
PASSÉ SIMP.	il **naquit**, ils naquirent
IMPERF.	je **naiss**ais, etc.
PRES. PART.	naissant

offrir *to offer, like* **ouvrir**

PRES. IND.	j'**offre**, tu offres, il offre, nous offrons, vous offrez, ils offrent
PASSÉ COMP.	j'ai **offert**

ouvrir *to open*

PRES. IND.	j'**ouvre**, tu ouvres, il ouvre, nous ouvrons, vous ouvrez, ils ouvrent
PRES. SUBJ.	j'**ouvre**, tu ouvres, il ouvre, nous ouvrions, vous ouvriez, ils ouvrent
FUT.	j'**ouvrir**ai, etc.
CONDIT.	j'**ouvrir**ais, etc.
PASSÉ COMP.	j'ai **ouvert**, etc.
PASSÉ SIMP.	il **ouvrit**, ils ouvrirent
IMPERF.	j'**ouvr**ais, etc.
PRES. PART.	ouvrant

paraître *to seem, like* **connaître**

PRES. IND.	je **parais**, tu parais, il paraît, nous **paraiss**ons, vous paraissez, ils paraissent
PASSÉ COMP.	j'ai **paru**, etc.

partir *to leave*

PRES. IND.	je **par**s, tu pars, il part, nous **part**ons, vous partez, ils partent
PRES. SUBJ.	je **part**e, tu partes, il parte, nous partions, vous partiez, ils partent
FUT.	je **partir**ai, etc.
CONDIT.	je **partir**ais, etc.

PASSÉ COMP.	je suis **parti(e)**, etc.
PASSÉ SIMP.	il partit, ils partirent
IMPERF.	je **part**ais, etc.
PRES. PART.	partant

peindre *to paint, like* **craindre**

| PRES. IND. | je **pein**s, tu peins, il peint, nous **peign**ons, vous peignez, ils peignent |
| PASSÉ COMP. | j'ai **peint**, etc. |

perdre *to lose, like* **vendre**

| PRES. IND. | je **perd**s, tu perds, il perd, nous **perd**ons, vous perdez, ils perdent |
| PASSÉ COMP. | j'ai **perdu**, etc. |

permettre *to permit, see* **mettre**

plaindre *to pity, like* **craindre**

| PRES. IND. | je **plain**s, tu plains, il plaint, nous **plaign**ons, vous plaignez, ils plaignent |
| PASSÉ COMP. | j'ai **plaint**, etc. |

plaire *to please*

PRES. IND.	je **plais**, tu plais, il plaît, nous **plais**ons, vous plaisez, ils plaisent
PRES. SUBJ.	je **plais**e, tu plaises, il plaise, nous plaisions, vous plaisiez, ils plaisent
FUT.	je **plair**ai, etc.
CONDIT.	je **plair**ais, etc.
PASSÉ COMP.	j'ai **plu**, etc.
PASSÉ SIMP.	il plut, ils plurent
IMPERF.	je **plais**ais, etc.
PRES. PART.	plaisant

pleuvoir *to rain (impersonal)*

PRES. IND.	il **pleu**t
PRES. SUBJ.	il **pleuv**e
FUT.	il **pleuv**ra
CONDIT.	il **pleuv**rait
PASSÉ COMP.	il a **plu**
PASSÉ SIMP.	il plut
IMPERF.	il **pleuv**ait
PRES. PART.	pleuvant

pouvoir *to be able*

PRES. IND.	je **peux**[1], tu peux, il peut, nous **pouv**ons, vous pouvez, ils **peuv**ent
PRES. SUBJ.	je **puiss**e, tu puisses, il puisse, nous puissions, vous puissiez, ils puissent
FUT.	je **pourr**ai, etc.
CONDIT.	je **pourr**ais, etc.
PASSÉ COMP.	j'ai **pu**, etc.
PASSÉ SIMP.	il put, ils purent
IMPERF.	je **pouv**ais, etc.
PRES. PART.	pouvant

prendre *to take*

PRES. IND.	je **prend**s, tu prends, il prend, nous **pren**ons, vous prenez, ils **prenn**ent
PRES. SUBJ.	je **prenn**e, tu prennes, il prenne, nous **pren**ions, vous preniez, ils **prenn**ent
FUT.	je **prendr**ai, etc.
CONDIT.	je **prendr**ais, etc.
PASSÉ COMP.	j'ai **pris**, etc.

---

1. Interrogative: **puis-je?**

PASSÉ SIMP.	il prit, ils prirent
IMPERF.	je **pren**ais, etc.
PRES. PART.	prenant

recevoir *to receive*

PRES. IND.	je **reçoi**s, tu reçois, il reçoit, nous **recev**ons, vous recevez, ils **reçoiv**ent
PRES. SUBJ.	je **reçoiv**e, tu reçoives, il reçoive, nous **recevi**ons, vous receviez, ils **reçoiv**ent
FUT.	je **recevr**ai, etc.
CONDIT.	je **recevr**ais, etc.
PASSÉ COMP.	j'ai **reçu**, etc.
PASSÉ SIMP.	il reçut, ils reçurent
IMPERF.	je **recev**ais, etc.
PRES. PART.	recevant

rejoindre *to rejoin, like* **craindre**

| PRES. IND. | je **rejoin**s, tu rejoins, il rejoint, nous **rejoign**ons, vous rejoignez, ils rejoignent |
| PASSÉ COMP. | j'ai **rejoint**, etc. |

répondre *to answer, like* **vendre**

| PRES. IND. | je **répond**s, tu réponds, il répond, nous **répond**ons, vous répondez, ils répondent |
| PASSÉ COMP. | j'ai **répond**u, etc. |

rire *to laugh*

PRES. IND.	je **ri**s, tu ris, il rit, nous rions, vous riez, ils rient
PRES. SUBJ.	je **ri**e, tu ries, il rie, nous riions, vous riiez, ils rient
FUT.	je **rir**ai, etc.
CONDIT.	je **rir**ais, etc.
PASSÉ COMP.	j'ai **ri**, etc.
PASSÉ SIMP.	il rit, ils rirent
IMPERF.	je **ri**ais, etc.
PRES. PART.	riant

rompre *to break, like* **vendre** *but with* **p** *in present tense and stem*

| PRES. IND. | je **romp**s, tu romps, il rompt, nous **romp**ons, vous rompez, ils rompent |
| PASSÉ COMP. | j'ai **romp**u, etc. |

savoir *to know*

PRES. IND.	je **sai**s, tu sais, il sait, nous **sav**ons, vous savez, ils savent
PRES. SUBJ.	je **sach**e, tu saches, il sache, nous sachions, vous sachiez, ils sachent
FUT.	je **saur**ai, etc.
CONDIT.	je **saur**ais, etc.
PASSÉ COMP.	j'ai **su**, etc.
PASSÉ SIMP.	il **sut**, ils surent
IMPERF.	je **sav**ais, etc.
PRES. PART.	sachant
IMPERATIVE	**sach**e, sachons, sachez

sentir *to feel, like* **partir**

| PRES. IND. | je **sen**s, tu sens, il sent, nous **sent**ons, vous sentez, ils sentent |
| PASSÉ COMP. | j'ai **senti**, etc. |

servir *to serve, like* **partir**

| PRES. IND. | je **ser**s, tu sers, il sert, nous **serv**ons, vous servez, ils servent |
| PASSÉ COMP. | j'ai **servi**, etc. |

sortir *to go out, leave, like* **partir**

| PRES. IND. | je **sor**s, tu sors, il sort, nous **sort**ons, vous sortez, ils sortent |
| PASSÉ COMP. | je suis **sorti(e)**, etc. |

souffrir *to suffer, like* **ouvrir**

PRES IND.	je **souffr**e, tu souffres, il souffre, nous souffrons, vous souffrez, ils souffrent
PASSÉ COMP.	j'ai **souffert**, etc.

se souvenir *to remember, like* **venir**

PRES. IND.	je me **souvien**s, tu te souviens, il se souvient, nous nous **souven**ons, vous vous souvenez, ils se **souvienn**ent
PASSÉ COMP.	je me suis **souvenu(e)**, etc.

suffire *to suffice*

PRES. IND.	je **suffi**s, tu suffis, il suffit, nous **suffis**ons, vous suffisez, ils suffisent
PRES. SUBJ.	je **suffis**e, tu suffises, il suffise, nous suffisions, vous suffisiez, ils suffisent
FUT.	je **suffir**ai, etc.
CONDIT.	je **suffir**ais, etc.
PASSÉ COMP.	j'ai **suffi**, etc.
PASSÉ SIMP.	il suffit, ils suffirent
IMPERF.	je **suffis**ais, etc.
PRES. PART.	suffisant

suivre *to follow*

PRES. IND.	je **sui**s, tu suis, il suit, nous **suiv**ons, vous suivez, ils suivent
PRES. SUBJ.	je **suiv**e, tu suives, il suive, nous suivions, vous suiviez, ils suivent
FUT.	je **suivr**ai, etc.
CONDIT.	je **suivr**ais, etc.
PASSÉ COMP.	j'ai **suivi**, etc.
PASSÉ SIMP.	il suivit, ils suivirent
IMPERF.	je **suiv**ais, etc.
PRES. PART.	suivant

se taire *to keep silent, like* **plaire**, *but no circumflex accent*

PRES. IND.	je me **tai**s, tu te tais, il se tait, nous nous **tais**ons, vous vous taisez, ils se taisent
PASSÉ COMP.	je me suis **tu(e)**, etc.

tenir *to hold, like* **venir**

PRES. IND.	je **tien**s, tu tiens, il tient, nous **ten**ons, vous tenez, ils **tienn**ent
PASSÉ COMP.	j'ai **tenu**, etc.

traduire *to translate, like* **conduire**

PRES. IND.	je **tradui**s, tu traduis, il traduit, nous **tradui**sons, vous traduisez, ils traduisent
PASSÉ COMP.	j'ai **traduit**, etc.

valoir *to be worth*

PRES. IND.	je **vau**x, tu vaux, il vaut, nous **val**ons, vous valez, ils valent
PRES. SUBJ.	je **vaill**e, tu vailles, il vaille, nous **val**ions, vous valiez, ils **vaill**ent
FUT.	je **vaudr**ai, etc.
CONDIT.	je **vaudr**ais, etc.
PASSÉ COMP.	j'ai **valu**, etc.
PASSÉ SIMP.	il valut, ils valurent
IMPERF.	je **val**ais, etc.
PRES. PART.	valant

venir *to come*

PRES. IND.	je **vien**s, tu viens, il vient, nous **ven**ons, vous venez, ils **vienn**ent
PRES. SUBJ.	je **vienn**e, tu viennes, il vienne, nous **ven**ions, vous veniez, ils **vienn**ent
FUT.	je **viendr**ai, etc.
CONDIT.	je **viendr**ais, etc.
PASSÉ COMP.	je suis **venu(e)**, etc.
PASSÉ SIMP.	il **vint**, ils vinrent

| IMPERF. | je **ven**ais, etc. |
| PRES. PART. | venant |

vivre *to live*

PRES. IND.	je **vis**, tu vis, il vit, nous **viv**ons, vous vivez, ils vivent
PRES. SUBJ.	je **viv**e, tu vives, il vive, nous vivions, vous viviez, ils vivent
FUT.	je **vivr**ai, etc.
CONDIT.	je **vivr**ais, etc.
PASSÉ COMP.	j'ai **vécu**, etc.
PASSÉ SIMP.	il vécut, ils vécurent
IMPERF.	je **viv**ais, etc.
PRES. PART.	vivant

voir *to see*

PRES. IND.	je **voi**s, tu vois, il voit, nous **voy**ons, vous voyez, ils **voi**ent
PRES. SUBJ.	je **voi**e, tu voies, il voie, nous **voy**ions, vous voyiez, ils **voi**ent
FUT.	je **verr**ai, etc.
CONDIT.	je **verr**ais, etc.
PASSÉ COMP.	j'ai **vu**, etc.
PASSÉ SIMP.	il **vit**, ils virent
IMPERF.	je **voy**ais, etc.
PRES. PART.	voyant

vouloir *to want*

PRES. IND.	je **veux**, tu veux, il veut, nous **voul**ons, vous voulez, ils **veul**ent
PRES. SUBJ.	je **veuill**e, tu veuilles, il veuille, nous **voul**ions, vous vouliez, ils **veuill**ent
FUT.	je **voudr**ai, etc.
CONDIT.	je **voudr**ais, etc.
PASSÉ COMP.	j'ai **voulu**, etc.
PASSÉ SIMP.	il voulut, ils voulurent
IMPERF.	je **voul**ais, etc.
PRES. PART.	voulant
IMPERATIVE	**veuillez**

Numbers
(Nombres)

1	un, une		41	quarante et un
2	deux		42	quarante-deux, *etc.*
3	trois		50	cinquante
4	quatre		51	cinquante et un
5	cinq		52	cinquante-deux, *etc.*
6	six		60	soixante
7	sept		61	soixante et un
8	huit		62	soixante-deux, *etc.*
9	neuf		70	soixante-dix
10	dix		71	soixante et onze
11	onze		72	soixante-douze
12	douze		73	soixante-treize
13	treize		74	soixante-quatorze
14	quatorze		75	soixante-quinze
15	quinze		76	soixante-seize
16	seize		77	soixante-dix-sept
17	dix-sept		78	soixante-dix-huit
18	dix-huit		79	soixante-dix-neuf
19	dix-neuf		80	quatre-vingts
20	vingt		81	quatre-vingt-un
21	vingt et un		82	quatre-vingt-deux
22	vingt-deux		83	quatre-vingt-trois, *etc.*
23	vingt-trois		90	quatre-vingt-dix
24	vingt-quatre		91	quatre-vingt-onze
25	vingt-cinq		92	quatre-vingt-douze
26	vingt-six		93	quatre-vingt-treize, *etc.*
27	vingt-sept		100	cent
28	vingt-huit		101	cent un
29	vingt-neuf		200	deux cents
30	trente		201	deux cent un
31	trente et un		1000	mille
32	trente-deux		1001	mille un
33	trente-trois		2000	deux mille
34	trente-quatre, *etc.*		1 000 000	un million
40	quarante		1 000 000 000	un milliard